KNOW WHY
YOU BELIEVE

K. SCOTT OLIPHINT

JUSTIN S. HOLCOMB, SERIES EDITOR

Books in the Know Series

KNOW
WHY YOU
BELIEVE

K. SCOTT OLIPHINT

JUSTIN S. HOLCOMB, SERIES EDITOR

ZONDERVAN

Know Why You Believe
Copyright © 2017 by K. Scott Oliphint

This title is also available as a Zondervan ebook.

Requests for information should be addressed to:
Zondervan, *3900 Sparks Dr. SE, Grand Rapids, Michigan 49546*

ISBN 978-0-310-52597-4

Art direction: Gearbox
Interior design: Greg Johnson/Textbook Perfect

Printed in the United States of America

17 18 19 20 21 22 23 24 25 /DCI/ 15 14 13 12 11 10 9 8 7 6 5 4 3 2

To Kyle, Lizzie, Katie, Caroline, and Kelly

CONTENTS

ACKNOWLEDGMENTS

I would like to thank Justin Holcomb for his kind invitation to write this book and his guidance in its beginning stages. I would also like to thank Madison Trammel at Zondervan for his help and encouragement along the way.

Special thanks to my niece, Katie Oliphint, who patiently read and offered helpful comments on the bulk of this book.

INTRODUCTION

> I believe in Christianity as I believe that the sun has risen: not
> only because I see it, but because by it I see everything else.
> —C. S. Lewis

Toward the end of World War II, C. S. Lewis delivered a lecture
to the Oxford Socratic Club titled "Is Theology Poetry?" The
epigraph to this introduction is taken from that lecture.[1] Only
Christianity can shed light on everything we think, ask, live, or
do. This is Lewis's succinct response to the question, "Why Christianity?" In one short statement, he says volumes.

Any parent knows the *why* question can become exhausting.
Children have an innate ability to ask it—over and over again.
They're not taught to ask it. Parents spend no time instructing
them about the meaning and importance of asking it. Children
just by nature ask it and ask it and ask it again.

Why do children instinctively ask why? Answering this question
could never end. If we answer by saying, "Children instinctively
ask why because it is in their nature to do so," it raises another
question: "But why is it in their nature?" And on and on it could go.

The reason the *why* question begins at an early age is because
we are interested in the reasons for the things in our world. We
ask the *why* question for mental and practical relaxation. What
we are after in asking why is a place of rest. We want to be able to
live our lives, do our work, watch the news, and relate to others,

all the while recognizing the meaning of what we're doing and why we're doing it. We want more than simply to do things. We want to understand things.

This is why Lewis's quote is so striking. It is a sweeping conclusion to the *why* question. Christianity, for Lewis, is not simply one thing among many things he believes. Instead, he is saying that he believes in Christianity *because* it enables him to see everything in a proper light.

Christianity is a way of seeing. It provides a foundation for everything we think, do, and believe. It gives a proper perspective on us and on the rest of the world.

Think of reciting the Apostles' Creed:

> I believe in God, the Father Almighty, the Maker of heaven and earth, and in Jesus Christ, his only Son, our Lord; who was conceived by the Holy Ghost, born of the Virgin Mary, suffered under Pontius Pilate, was crucified, dead, and buried. He descended into hell. The third day he arose again from the dead. He ascended into heaven and sitteth on the right hand of God the Father Almighty, from thence he shall come to judge the quick and the dead. I believe in the Holy Ghost, the holy catholic church, the communion of saints, the forgiveness of sins, the resurrection of the body, and the life everlasting. Amen.[2]

The question is, "*Why* do we believe those things?"

The following chapters discuss why Christians believe what we do. The chapters also include objections from those who challenge our reasons for believing what we do. At the end of each chapter are questions to expand understanding of the reasons we gave, followed by suggestions for further reading.

The source of the topics we will discuss is the Bible. Everything we discuss in this book depends on how we view the Bible. The first chapter in this book is foundational.

We can trust the Bible to give us truth. The Bible not only is the source of what Christians believe, but it also points us to everything else in the world—and beyond! It points us to the way the world is, to who we are, and, most important, to who God is.

We could think of the Bible as the eyeglasses through which we see everything. If our eyesight is poor, no matter how wide we open our eyes, we do not have a clear view of the things we see. But through the 20/20 vision of the Bible, we can see clearly.[3]

Christianity is not a religion that has its primary source in nature, or in experience, or even in an individual's salvation. The source for Christianity is the Revealer, Jesus himself, who has much to say about nature, experience, and salvation. Our salvation is not something we can earn through works or that we deserve. Christianity comes to us as a gift from God.

The Christian religion stretches all the way back to the beginning of time, where Scripture began. Christianity encompasses the entire history of redemption before the time of Christ, and it tells us a good deal about what we can expect now and in the future.

This is why the quote from C. S. Lewis is so helpful: "I believe in Christianity as I believe that the sun has risen: not only because I see it, but because by it I see everything else." Christians today don't believe Christianity because they've seen Christ, or his miracles, or his resurrection, or God. Christians believe because of the testimony given to us in the Bible. And through Christianity we are able to properly see everything.

We begin the book with a discussion of the various things the Bible teaches—about God, about Jesus, about miracles, about life after death. We also show how we should think about the Bible's teachings in light of what science is telling us about our world. Each of these topics deserves an entire book. We establish some of the main things that need to be considered in light of the Christian faith.

We make one concession: There is no amount of evidence, or discussion, or argument that will, by itself, change anyone's mind to a belief in Christianity. Christianity is a religion of faith, knowledgable faith. Christianity is properly understood only by knowing and trusting in Jesus Christ.

We also offer one challenge: While reading this book, there may be things you simply cannot believe. If so, ask yourself this question: "What am I trusting in that will not allow me to believe this?" We all trust in something—or in some things.

The most important question throughout this book will be, "Do *I* believe this, and, if not, why don't I believe *this*?"

CHAPTER 1

WHY BELIEVE IN THE BIBLE?

It was the wee hours of the morning. I couldn't sleep, so decided to see if the television might lull me to sleep. I happened on an infomercial touting the "amazing success" of a vibrating device that fit around your waist and was supposed to shrink your waist by inches! The results this device was supposed to deliver were unbelievable, literally. The success of sales commercials like this one has surely diminished now that we can go online and read reviews from users.

The infomercial prompted a few questions. Why is such an amazing device sold only through a television commercial? At 3:00 a.m.? Why wouldn't the inventor sell it in prime time? Why not put them in every store in the country? Why don't I know anyone who uses this device? There was no hint that the device was new. Yet I had never heard of it. There was something amazing about this device—the amazing inconsistency between its supposed success and the way it was being sold.

People are tempted to treat the Bible like this infomercial. Skeptical questions arise quickly. How credible are the Bible's claims? Are there people who believe it? Is it too obscure to be read by most people? Is it the equivalent of a product promoted on TV at 3:00 a.m.?

A quick look at reviews of the English Standard Version of the Bible on Amazon.com reveals two examples: "Better for Arabian nights than actual spirituality. Contradicts itself in the first two sections and it's racist, encourages slavery, bigoted and generally makes no sense." Another reviewer says the Bible is "neither accurate nor truthful."

These reviews make the Bible sound like an infomercial. What it says is incoherent, not to mention offensive; it's neither accurate nor truthful.

Despite these bad reviews, the Bible's track record is strong. According to the Guinness Book of World Records, the Bible remains the bestselling book of all time. Estimates are that more than seven billion copies have been sold. No other book even comes close. The Bible has been translated into more than 350 languages, making it accessible to billions of people around the world. It is difficult to think that a book that is "neither accurate nor truthful" would amass the popularity the Bible has over so many years.

Why is the Bible so popular?

Reasons

The reasons for believing the Bible are formidable. For the sake of clarity, we will divide these reasons into external and internal. The external reasons are those that come from outside of the Bible itself, such as the historical evidence that attests to the Bible's history. The internal reasons, which are more definitive, are those that the Bible itself contains.

External Reasons

When we ask the question, "Why believe the Bible?" we are asking a specific kind of question, a question that has many sides to it. It might be useful to ask the question this way: "What would it take for me to believe that what the Bible says is true?" When the question is put like this, it becomes more personal.

Believing in what the Bible says is not like believing that water freezes at 32 degrees Fahrenheit. We can set up the right conditions to demonstrate the truth that water freezes at 32 degrees. We can repeat the demonstration anytime, any place. People can see the water freeze and believe the truth of the statement.

Believing that the Bible is true is not simple. Would you believe the Bible is true if you were certain it is historically accurate? Christianity, unlike other world religions and many cults, is not the product of one person or of one secret meeting or of a private revelation, as is the case, for example, with Islam, Mormonism, and Jehovah's Witnesses. Christianity is not a private religion. It is a public religion embedded in the history of the world.

Christianity is a religion with historical documentation that extends back through Judaism to the beginning of time. Much of Christianity's history took place in a relatively small part of the world—the Middle East. The Bible names cities and countries and regions, many of which still exist today. Archeology continues to unearth the remains of extinct cities, places, and cultures mentioned in the Bible. For example, the Bible states in three different books that King Hezekiah reigned over Judah (2 Kings 17–20; Isa. 36–39; 2 Chron. 29–32). Recently, an archeological dig in Jerusalem discovered a seal that belonged to him with the inscription, "Belonging to Hezekiah, [son of] Ahaz king of Judah."[1]

That inscripted seal provides proof of the historical nature of the Old Testament.

Archeology keeps adding more and more support to the Old Testament narratives. In the 1990s, an inscription was found that confirmed the existence of "the house of King David," which is discussed in the books of the Old Testament.

Regarding the history of the New Testament, there are at least three records describing the existence of Jesus Christ and his followers done by men outside of Christianity. One is from Jewish historian Josephus (c. AD 37), who wrote that Jesus was a man who did wondrous works and whose followers said he was the Messiah. Josephus also recorded the fact that Jesus was put to death by Pilate. Tacitus (c. AD 56–120), also not a Christian, described the first-century persecution of Christians. He attributed the Christian movement to Jesus Christ, a Jew who was killed under Pontius Pilate. A man named Pliny (c. AD 61–112) recorded the continuation of Christianity into the second century. He wrote that Christians were meeting weekly to worship Christ as if he were God.[2]

These are remarkable factual records from men who were not part of the Christian movement. In their writing, Josephus, Tacitus, and Pliny recorded some central and crucial Christian teachings and beliefs, including the fact that his followers believed that Jesus was the Messiah, the Christ, and long after his death on the cross, worshiped him as if he was God. A multitude of historical and cultural evidence shows the historical consistency of the Old and New Testaments.

For those looking for reasons to believe the Bible, however, this evidence can seem to be too weak, unconvincing.

The question, "What would it take for me to believe the Bible is true?" needs more than just historical records and objects. "Granted there are historical testimonies to the Bible's history," you might say, "but what about the books that are included in the Bible? Is it possible to confirm their accuracy?"

With respect to the Old Testament, much of its confirmation can be found in the New Testament. From Jesus to his apostles, the attribution of authority and divinity to the Old Testament is beyond doubt. As for external testimonies to its authority, the discovery from about 1946 to 1956, of various caves in the West Bank that contained what we call the Dead Sea Scrolls, added significant and substantial support for the reliability of the Old Testament. Of the eleven or so caves containing ancient manuscripts, Cave 5 housed what is thought to be the oldest Hebrew manuscript, a fragment of the book of Samuel from the third century BC. The cave also contained a hundred copies of various books of the Bible, adding up to the entire Old Testament except Esther.[3] In addition to the manuscripts found in the caves near the Dead Sea, there are thousands of other manuscripts that confirm the accuracy of the words given in the Old Testament.

What about the New Testament?

The sheer number of manuscripts available to confirm the New Testament is overwhelming, when compared with similar documents. Counting only texts written in Greek, there are at present 5,686 manuscripts that copy part or all of the New Testament, some dating perhaps to the first century![4] By contrast, the second most documented work from this time period is Homer's *Iliad*, which has 646 supporting manuscripts. Other works have far fewer manuscripts. There are only ten copies of Julius Caesar's *Gallic War*, eight copies of Thucydides's *History*, and only two copies of the *Annals* by Tacitus.

The thousands of manuscripts of the books of the Bible lend credence to the material in the Bible. Unlike so many other books that we count as real history, there are copies and more copies, extending through centuries, that all confirm the contents of the Bible.

But maybe you need more evidence. Maybe you need to know how it was determined that the books in the Bible are the right ones. Perhaps you need an answer to the question, "Who decided which books would be in and which would be out?"

Questions like this tend to center on the books of the New Testament. When we begin to address the question of the included books, or canon, of the New Testament, we are moving much closer to the central focus of our "why believe" question.

In a dialogue between two characters, Leigh Teabing and Sophie Saint-Clair, Dan Brown, in his popular book (and later movie) *The Da Vinci Code*, writes this about the origin of the Gospels and of Christianity:

> [Teabing:] "The Bible is a product of *man*, my dear. Not of God. The Bible did not fall magically from the clouds. Man created it as a historical record of tumultuous times, and it has evolved through countless translations, additions, and revisions. History has never had a definitive version of the book."
>
> [Sophie:] "Okay."
>
> [Teabing:] ". . . More than *eighty* gospels were considered for the New Testament, and yet only a relatively few were chosen . . ."
>
> [Sophie:] "Who chose which gospels to include?"

[Teabing: (with enthusiasm)] "Aha! The fundamental
  irony of Christianity! The Bible as we know it
  today, was collated by the pagan Roman emperor
  Constantine the Great."[5]

As anyone who was around during the release of this book
and movie can testify, *The Da Vinci Code* garnered an enormous
audience and created a new generation of Bible skeptics.

The problem with the Teabing and Sophie discussion is serious. It has no basis in fact. The notion that Emperor Constantine
collated the books of the New Testament could not be further
from the truth. Any cursory glance at the writings of the second-
century church fathers, before Constantine was even on the scene,
shows that the books of the New Testament were already in use
and affirmed by the Christian churches in the East and in the
West. Constantine, who was responsible for calling the Council
at Nicea in 325 AD, was as dependent on the completed canon of
the New Testament as anyone else in the fourth century.[6] There
is not one shred of historical evidence for anything that Brown
asserts. Nevertheless, for those who would rather remain skeptics
than look at history, Brown's book provided new fuel.

There never was a council called to decide which books to
include in the New Testament. This might seem strange since
it is clear that many councils were called periodically to decide
substantial doctrinal issues in the church.[7] Why would there be
no council to decide something as fundamental as what books to
include in the New Testament?

One answer to this question has to do with the conditions
that prompted councils and assemblies to be called in the first
place. These historic assemblies were not called because various

church leaders were simply interested in developing their theology. Rather, these councils needed to meet to avert and respond to serious doctrinal error in the church.

The Council of Nicea (325 AD), for example, was called by Emperor Constantine to affirm the identity and full deity of Jesus Christ against the position of Arius and his followers, who argued, with some success, that Christ, while in some ways unique, was not fully God. A little more than a hundred years later, a council had to be called at Chalcedon to discuss and affirm the two natures in the one person of Jesus Christ. Nicea opposed Arianism; Chalcedon opposed Eutychianism (that Christ had one nature) and Nestorianism (that Christ was two personalities). Oftentimes sound doctrine developed in the church in the face of controversy and error.

No council was needed to decide which books to include in the New Testament. The church understood and recognized from its earliest days which books contained the authority of Christ and which did not. Though there were those who opposed the acceptance of the books, such as Marcion,[8] those detractors were seen as renegades who were at odds with what the church had already recognized about the books of the New Testament.

The early church received these new books, which eventually were called the New Testament. The great Princeton theologian B. B. Warfield wrote,

> They received new book after new book from the apostolical circle, as equally "Scripture" with the old books, and added them one by one to the collection of old books as additional Scriptures, until at length the new books thus added were numerous enough to be looked upon as another *section* of the Scriptures.[9]

Internal Reasons

Christians can remain skeptical despite the historical and manuscript evidence that supports the Bible's historical integrity. That is a natural reaction. As one author put it, "From a strictly evidential perspective, we cannot be absolutely certain of what books are in the canon and whether the canon is closed. *Historical evidence as such provides only probability, not certainty.*"[10] External evidence will always remain inconclusive. This means that the best we can do with external evidence is "maybe, but maybe not."

The reason goes back to our illustration of the freezing point of water. The external evidence that water freezes at 32 degrees Fahrenheit is conclusive. For anyone who doesn't believe it, you can set up a demonstration and prove its truth, and you can demonstrate it over and over again.

Christianity is not like that. Christianity's proof runs much deeper and is much more sweeping than what any scientific or historical evidence can show. Christianity is not simply about a historical book. It has its focus in a person, the Lord Jesus Christ. A discussion of how we can believe the Bible is true cannot be left simply with history. It has to involve, first and foremost, a relationship with Jesus.

Believing that the Bible is true is more like being in a marriage relationship than like a scientific experiment. Typically, when a man is interested in getting married to a woman, he will go through a period of engagement with her. This period is akin to gathering external evidence of what living with that person would be like. However, no matter how long the engagement, there can be no marriage relationship until the commitment is made and living together as a married couple begins. Only then will one know what marriage is like. A commitment is required before the reality of marriage can be understood in its fullness. No book can do that; no amount of evidence can produce that reality. Only the marriage commitment can do it.

So it is with Christianity. It makes perfect sense to try to get to know Christianity from the outside. But all we have available are probabilities and speculations. Only a personal commitment to Christ brings to light what Christianity actually is.

The persuasive reasons for believing the Bible is true have to do with the character of the book itself. Unlike any other literary work, the 66 books of the Bible were written by many different people over a period of approximately 1,500 years. With such a diversity, it's natural to think that the Bible would contain a diversity of religious ideas and truths. This is why so many cults focus their religion in one person and one short period of time. It's much easier that way. But Christianity has never seen such diversity as a weakness. The diversity of the Bible is further testimony of its truth.

Historically, the internal evidence of the Bible's truth is focused on the unity of its diversity. For example, the *Westminster Confession of Faith* gives a partial list of arguments as evidence that the Bible is God's Word. Those arguments include

> the heavenliness of the matter, the efficacy of the doctrine, the majesty of the style, the consent of all the parts, the scope of the whole (which is, to give all glory to God), the full discovery it makes of the only way of man's salvation, the many other incomparable excellencies, and the entire perfection thereof.[11]

All of this internal evidence requires familiarity with the content of Scripture, not just its history. One must sit down and read what the Bible says. It doesn't matter where you begin to read. If there is in Scripture a "consent of all the parts," then wherever one begins will be consistent with other books and passages one reads along the way.

But let's say you open the Bible and begin at the beginning. The first thing you will read is, "In the beginning God created the heavens and the earth" (Gen. 1:1). Immediately you will be aware of what the Confession calls "the heavenliness of the matter." The Bible is not a history book. It is a book given and written in history, but its subject matter is more heavenly than historical. It begins with creation.

But creation is not the beginning of all that exists. Even in the beginning, God already existed. In the first words of the Bible, we read of him who transcends, even as he establishes, all of creation. From beginning to end, the Bible points us beyond ourselves and beyond our existence to heaven itself, where God, who is not earthly, has always been.

By the "efficacy of the doctrine," the Confession is pointing us to the application of what Scripture teaches to the lives of people given to us in the Bible. Throughout the Bible, we see God in relation with human beings, calling them to various tasks, enlisting their services to accomplish his purposes. Through all of Scripture, God graciously offers life. When, as with Adam, the decision is made to forego that life and to choose death instead, God steps in and provides a way for life to overcome the death that is now the natural condition of all people (see Gen. 3:15). What God does in Scripture and promises throughout Scripture since the time when Adam brought God's good creation under a curse, all point to one event—the coming of God the Son in the person of Jesus Christ. The "efficacy of the doctrine" means that what God teaches and proclaims throughout Scripture comes to pass. It all has its focus in God's condescension, his "coming down" to save and redeem. That focus reaches its climactic goal in the coming of the Son of God in the flesh.

By the "majesty of the style," the Confession highlights the transcendent character of the truth of Scripture. Unlike the truth of the freezing point of water, the truth of Scripture points us outward and upward, beyond creation, to the very dwelling place of God. (See, for example, Ps. 90:1.) Once we grasp and own the truths of Scripture, the very style of those sixty-six books moves us to a life beyond ourselves, to the life that is found only in God through his Son.

These and other arguments are given in the Bible to move those who read it and believe it to a certainty about the truth of the Bible and about the one whose truth it is. We cannot grasp and own these truths simply by our intellectual efforts. Even if all of the arguments in the Confession were given, more is needed. The Confession concludes with this: "Yet notwithstanding, our full persuasion and assurance of the infallible truth and divine authority thereof, is from the inward work of the Holy Spirit bearing witness by and with the Word in our hearts."

Whenever we contemplate why we believe the Bible, or whenever we attempt to give reasons for our belief in Scripture, this last and deeply personal affirmation of the work of the Holy Spirit in us must be recognized. The only way that one can be fully persuaded and assured of the "infallible truth and divine authority" of Holy Scripture is when the Holy Spirit himself testifies of the truth of Scripture in our hearts. That work always includes his "bearing witness" of the truth and efficacy of what the Bible says. (We will look more at this in chapter 6.)

We should not miss this most important point. The Holy Spirit does not do his internal work by himself. Instead, he works "by and with the Word in our hearts." His work is accomplished only when we expose ourselves to the words of Scripture. The Spirit has seen fit to work with those words because it was he himself who, through human agency, produced them (see 2 Tim. 3:16). We must expose ourselves to what Scripture says. Only then can we hope to see the heavenliness, the majesty, the efficacy, the glory of God, and the entire perfection of Scripture. Without that exposure, the best answer to the *why* question is little more than a historical probability, and the power of what Scripture says can never be known.

Responses

"But," someone will object, "aren't you simply reasoning in a circle here? Aren't you telling me that the only reason to believe the Bible is because of what the Bible says about itself? Couldn't any book say the same thing about itself?"

This common objection stems from a misperception of the Christian understanding of the Bible. Suppose, for example, I asked you to prove to me, without in any way using your senses of sight or touch or hearing, that your senses were trustworthy guides for experiencing the world. How might you go about that? You can prove your senses to be reliable only by way of your senses.

There are no external sources that establish the reliability of the use of your senses.

The Christian understanding of the Bible is similar. One of the reasons that we spent some time looking at some external evidence concerning the Bible was to show that even though there is historical evidence for the Bible's reliability, such evidence says next to nothing about what the Bible is and how it can be affirmed as authoritative. For the Christian, the Bible, like our senses, is the only authoritative means we have for showing what it is. And because the Bible is the ultimate authority for Christians, there can be no other authority that can establish its authority. If another authority were to establish the Bible's authority, then the Bible would get its authority from something else and, by definition, would not be the final authority.

As for books of other religions (assuming this is a real objection and not just a red herring), it might be worthwhile to read those books, to look into the religions they support. Not only will those books pale in comparison with the rich and varied history of Scripture, but there will be no majesty, no efficacy, and, most important, no "full discovery of the only way of man's salvation,"[12] since salvation can only be accomplished by God himself! What other religion has been saying for millennia that only God can save us? All other religions place the burden of salvation on us, and it is a hopeless burden to carry.[13]

Another objection goes like this: "But what about all the contradictions in the Bible? How can you confess 'the consent of all the parts' and 'the entire perfection thereof' when the Bible is riddled with so many contradictions?"

Some have said that the Christian doctrine of the Trinity is a contradiction; some say the same about the doctrine of the incarnation. Or some will read the first three gospels and see, for example, that Jesus cleanses the temple toward the end of his ministry, but then read in the gospel of John that the temple cleansing was at the beginning. Are these not plain and obvious contradictions? Don't they present problems that inhibit any thinking person's belief in the Bible?

Reams have been written about this objection, and we can't deal with it in detail here. But maybe it will help to think of an analogy. You go to the doctor for a physical examination. At the conclusion of the exam, the doctor says, "I detected a problem with one of your organs, but this is what the human body is. It is nothing but a bunch of parts full of problems. It's no surprise that I found a problem in one part. See you next year." Obviously, you would find another doctor.

Any doctor committed to the profession begins with the proper notion that the human body is a coherent whole. All of the parts are meant to function in concert so that each part can function to its fullest. To diagnose problems in the body, you have to assume the harmony and consent of all the parts of the body working together.

So it is with Scripture. No one has exhausted the meaning of those sixty-six books; no one has the capacity to do so. The only way to diagnose perceived problems in Scripture is to study Scripture. When Scripture is studied with the commitment that the parts will be coherent because God is the primary author from beginning to end, contradictions disappear. But when Scripture is studied apart from that commitment, one encounters contradictions and problems because one begins with the premise that the Bible is full of contradictions.

Conclusion

When we consider a proper approach to the Bible, the marriage analogy can help us. The only way someone can acquire a "full persuasion and assurance of the infallible truth and divine authority" of Scripture is, as in marriage, by first making a commitment. That commitment is to Jesus Christ who is, through all of Scripture, "the only way of man's salvation."

This is one of the reasons the question was asked in this way: "What would it take for me to believe the Bible?" As a matter of fact, the Bible itself answers that question. It would take a "marriage" to Christ himself, and that marriage can only take place when one hears and *believes, trusts,* and owns what Scripture says. What it would take, in other words, is a work of the Holy Spirit in our hearts, as we read and as we trust Christ. Then we believe that what we read is the Word of God.

Once we believe and begin to read the Bible, we will affirm that we believe in Christ, not simply because we see him revealed in all of Scripture, but also because by believing him we are able properly to see everything else.

Here is the point we have to recognize as we progress through the rest of this book. *Unless we recognize these truths about the Bible, we will not be able to understand why we believe anything else about Christianity.* This point can hardly be overstated. These truths about Scripture will have to be our guide through the rest of this book. It could not be otherwise. It is the Holy Spirit who "fully persuades" us, through his own words in the Bible. The Bible presents to us "divine authority" about God, Jesus Christ, miracles, the resurrection, and everything else. So we can only discuss our "why" questions in the context of the answers that God himself gives to us, in his Word.

In trusting Christ and believing his Word, we begin to see the world and everything else in its proper light.

Questions for Reflection

1. Is the fact that the Bible was written over a period of sixteen centuries a strength or a weakness? Explain.
2. Some people have said that Christians worship a book. Is this what Christianity means when it says that the Bible is God's Word?
3. Since there never was a church council that agreed to put the right books in the New Testament, how can we be sure the books there are the right ones?
4. Like Scripture, what other authorities in our lives do we have to first trust before we can learn from them?

Recommended Reading

Garner, David B. *Did God Really Say? Affirming the Truth-fulness and Trustworthiness of Scripture*. Phillipsburg, NJ: P&R, 2012.

Grudem, Wayne, C. John Collins, and Thomas R. Schreiner. *Understanding Scripture: An Overview of the Bible's Origin, Reliability, and Meaning*. Wheaton, IL: Crossway, 2012.

MacArthur, John. *The Scripture Cannot Be Broken: Twentieth Century Writings on the Doctrine of Inerrancy*. Wheaton, IL: Crossway, 2015.

Packer, J. I. *God Has Spoken: Revelation and the Bible*. Grand Rapids: Baker, 1994.

Piper, John. *A Peculiar Glory: How the Christian Scriptures Reveal Their Complete Truthfulness*. Wheaton, IL: Crossway, 2016.

Ridderbos, Herman N. *Redemptive History and the New Testament Scriptures*. Biblical and Theological Studies. Phillipsburg, NJ: P&R, 1988.

Warfield, B. B. *The Inspiration and Authority of the Bible*. Phillipsburg, NJ: P&R, 1948.

CHAPTER 2

WHY BELIEVE IN GOD?

In the past couple of decades, there has been a resurgence of atheism. The New Atheists have presented various reasons why they find it impossible to believe in a god. Richard Dawkins, the late Christoper Hitchens, Sam Harris, and Daniel Dennett are considered the leaders of the New Atheism movement. Among Dawkins's books are *The God Delusion* (2006) and his earlier book, *The Selfish Gene* (1989). Hitchens's book *God Is Not Great: How Religion Poisons Everything* (2007) set him firmly in the New Atheism camp. Sam Harris is included in the group because of his *The End of Faith: Religion, Terror, and the Future of Reason* (2004) and *Letter to a Christian Nation* (2008). Daniel Dennett, the only philosopher of the four, wrote *Breaking the Spell: Religion as a Natural Phenomenon* (2006). These books flooded the publishing market at roughly the same time. The atheism promoted in each of the books motivated something of a "new" movement.

Reasons

Atheism, of course, is not new. Any perusal of the history of philosophy will show atheism to be a predominant theme in much of the literature. What's so "new" about the New Atheism? At least part of what is new is the boldness the authors exhibit in their rejection of a god. It is not just that they don't believe in a god. They are arguing that belief in a god is harmful to the perpetuation and flourishing of the human race. In other words, they are not simply making claims about their own belief. They are arguing that the rest of us should believe (or not believe) what they do about a god.

Reasons to Not Believe

For example, the late Christoper Hitchens, the most articulate of the four (in my opinion), in his book *God Is Not Great* titled the second chapter "Religion Kills." In that chapter he lists a host of religious abuses—including the Crusades, religious wars, personal abuses in the context of religion, religious people claiming supernatural powers—that would make any person, religious or not, ashamed. Hitchens was without peer in his ability to highlight the worst of religion, be it Christianity, Islam, or any other religion. Hitchens complains,

> The level of intensity fluctuates according to time and place, but it can be stated as a truth that religion does not, and in the long run cannot, be content with its own marvelous claims and sublime assurances. It *must* seek to interfere with the lives of nonbelievers, or heretics, or adherents of other faiths. It may speak about the bliss of the next world, but it wants power in this one. This is only to be expected. It is after all, wholly man-made. And it does not have the confidence in its own various preachings even to allow coexistence between different faiths.[1]

He begins this chapter with a quote from the philosopher Lucretius (99–55 BC): "To such heights of evil are men driven by religion." Hitchens is a master artist, able to paint all religions with such dark and menacing colors that almost anyone would question religion.

If we step back, however, and gain a little perspective on the picture Hitchens painted for us, we will begin to see that his painting will begin to look more like a "Where's Waldo?" In a "Where's Waldo?" picture, many things mimic various aspects of Waldo, but there is only one Waldo. The picture is ingeniously hiding the real thing.

Hitchens's depiction of religion is much like a "Where's Waldo?" Elements of his discussion resemble the real thing. But the real thing, Christianity, is too obscured and hidden to be accurately observed in anything he describes in the book.

Hitchens's tirade against religion is *not* about religion itself. What he discusses in the name of religion are the activities that religious people engaged in in the name of their religion. Though those activities might, in some ways, resemble elements of religion, they are not the real thing. After reading his descriptions, anyone interested in Christianity would ask, "But *where* is Christianity?" Descriptions of bad behavior by Christians is not Christianity.

When we're discussing Hitchens's arguments, we have to make a distinction that he neglected to make. We have to distinguish between what a religion is and what religious people do. In the context of Christianity, a distinction must be made between what Christianity is and what people who claim to be Christians do. We must also measure what Christians do in light of what Christianity is. Given Christianity's view of sin—its pervasiveness and horrendous effects in the world—it is illegitimate to equate the behavior of Christians with the truth that Christianity teaches.

No Christian would argue that anyone should believe in God based on Christian behavior. Instead, Christianity's belief in God is rooted in what God has done and said.

Richard Dawkins has many reasons why he doesn't want to believe in God. One reason has to do with the way he understands Scripture:

> The God of the Old Testament is arguably the most unpleasant character in all fiction: jealous and proud of it; a petty, unjust, unforgiving control-freak; a vindictive, blood-thirsty ethnic cleanser; a misogynistic, homophobic, racist, infanticidal, genocidal, filicidal, pestilential, megalomaniacal, sadomasochistic, capriciously malevolent bully.[2]

Obviously, there is a deep and disturbing bias controlling the way Dawkins understands the Old Testament.

Another aspect of Dawkins's atheism is focused on the things that are wrong in the world. Notice how he puts it:

> The total amount of suffering per year in the natural world is beyond all decent contemplation. . . . In a universe of blind physical forces and genetic replication, some people are going to get hurt, other people are going to get lucky, and you won't find any rhyme or reason in it, nor any justice. The universe that we observe has precisely the properties we should expect if there is, at bottom, no design, no purpose, no evil, no good, nothing but pitiless indifference.[3]

Dawkins rightly sees that there are terrible things in our world. We should expect things to be this terrible, he says, if there is no design or purpose or evil or good anywhere to be found in the world.

Dawkins, of course, is not able to make sense of his own analysis. If he really believed what he wrote, then a belief in the existence of God would be neither evil nor good; it would have no purpose or design. It would be as "indifferent" as his atheism. He shouldn't take the time to bother with it. But he does take the time—in provocative ways.

There is more complaining from Dawkins. Regarding those who don't believe that people randomly progressed from non-living matter, Dawkins says, "It is absolutely safe to say that if you meet somebody who claims not to believe in evolution, that person is ignorant, stupid or insane (or wicked, but I'd rather not consider that)."[4] Why should a denial of evolution be judged so harshly, given Dawkins's atheism? If reality is utterly indifferent, as Dawkins supposes, a denial of evolution is as indifferent as its affirmation. Dawkins would want us to believe that, in the end, nothing really matters. But his language shows that some things matter deeply to him. They matter so deeply he is willing to impugn the character of people who disagree with him.

Reasons to Believe

One of the most popular reasons given for believing in God is that most people do, and most people have, throughout human history. In a 2015 poll, the Barna Group found that only one in four people are atheists, skeptics, or agnostics. This means 75 percent of people believe in a god. By any estimation, when three quarters of a group believes something, it can be described as a dominant belief.[5]

This kind of reason for belief in God has been called a *consensus gentium* ("agreement of the people") argument. It was most famously set out by the orator Cicero (106–7 BC), who said, "There never was any nation so barbarous, nor any people in the world so savage, as to be without some notion of Gods."[6] Cicero's argument was repeated numerous times throughout history, including the history of the church.

John Calvin, to highlight just one example, in his discussion about the universal knowledge of God that resides in all people (more on this later), referred to Cicero in one of his writings:

> If ignorance of God is to be looked for anywhere, surely one is most likely to find an example of it among the more backward folk and those more remote from civilization. Yet there is, as the eminent pagan says, no nation so barbarous, no people so savage, that they have not a deep-seated conviction that there is a God.[7]

The "eminent pagan" to which Calvin refers here is Cicero.

The point of the "agreement of the people" argument is not that all people at all times and in all places have believed in a deity. There have always been some who disbelieve or who remain agnostic concerning belief in a god. The point is that there is a significant number, throughout history, who have professed belief in some kind of deity and who have therefore committed to some kind of religious ritual.

An "agreement of the people" argument might support the truth of a deity, but it is not sufficient to establish such a truth. The problem is a "significant number" of people who believe something is far from a proof. There was a time when a significant number of people believed the sun rotated around the earth. There was evidence for this belief, and people were able to make astronomical predictions while believing it. The belief was in error. Better evidence came to light, and better and more accurate predictions could be made when it was shown that the earth and the other planets revolve around the sun. The best an "agreement of the people" argument can offer is that the existence of a deity is probable, given what we know now. But no religious person should be content with the idea that God probably exists.

"Internal" Reasons

There have to be better reasons to believe in God than the "agreement of the people" argument. And there are.

One of the reasons that Calvin refers to Cicero, as in the previous quote, is not because Calvin thinks the "agreement of the people" argument is a strong and conclusive argument for God's existence. Instead, Calvin is explaining one of the reasons why most people, in every age, believe in some kind of deity.

The reason for this majority view is not that the majority of people have been given a conclusive proof for God's existence. Nor is it that the majority of people have studied the matter in depth. What Calvin rightly sees is that the "agreement of the people" is itself evidence of a deeper truth. This deeper truth Calvin calls the "sense of deity." He explains it this way:

> There is within the human mind, and indeed by natural instinct, an awareness of divinity. This we take to be beyond controversy. To prevent anyone from taking refuge in the pretense of ignorance, God himself has implanted in all men a certain understanding of his divine majesty. Ever renewing its memory, he repeatedly sheds fresh drops. Since, therefore, men one and all perceive that there is a God and that he is their Maker, they are condemned by their own testimony

because they have failed to honor him and to consecrate their lives to his will.[8]

When Calvin set out to write his *Institutes*, the topics that he chose to write about were determined by the topics that the apostle Paul discusses in the Epistle to the Romans. Calvin begins his book in the same way that Paul begins Romans—with the "Knowledge of God the Creator."

We have a natural instinct, which God himself has implanted in us, that includes a knowledge of God and an understanding of God's majesty. Calvin explains this through Paul's statement in the opening chapter of Romans (1:18–20):

> The wrath of God is being revealed from heaven against all the godlessness and wickedness of people, who suppress the truth by their wickedness, since what may be known about God is plain to them, because God has made it plain to them. For since the creation of the world God's invisible qualities— his eternal power and divine nature—have been clearly seen, being understood from what has been made, so that people are without excuse.

There is much to say about the Bible's teaching in these three verses, but we need only provide a summary of the crucial truths given in this passage.[9]

Paul's initial goal in Romans is to show that all people, both Jew and Gentile, are under the curse of sin (see Rom. 3:9). Each and every one of us is subject to the wrath of God (1:18). The picture Paul paints in our passage, however, is a picture that includes the "internal" process of our rebellion against God. God's wrath is his response to *our* response to him!

Paul, writing under the inspiration of the Holy Spirit, teaches us that our sin is what it is because of the fact that, as God's creatures, we all know him. The knowledge that we have of him is not a knowledge that is capable of saving us. For that we need knowledge of Christ and of his work. But the knowledge we have of God is, nevertheless, real and true knowledge of God the Creator (see Rom. 1:21).

The theological category often applied to Paul's discussion here is called God's "general revelation." General revelation is God's revelation that is constantly coming through all that he has made (see Ps. 19:1–8). That revelation, given by God, produces knowledge in us. It means that we all know God truly.

Our knowing God is not because, or if, we think properly about what we see, or because we are able to offer a conclusive proof for God's existence. Paul has no such thing in mind in this passage. Instead, we know God through what he has made because "God has made it plain to [us]" (Rom. 1:19). In other words, God is revealing himself through what he has made, and that revelation gets through to us. God does not fail in his task to make himself known to those who are made in his image.

God implants this truth in us through what he has made. It renders each and every one of us "without excuse." No one will stand before God on the day of judgment and say, "I didn't know you," or "You never showed me who you were." All of God's human creatures know his "invisible qualities—his eternal power and divine nature" (v. 20).

This is why Calvin says that God has "implanted" this sense of deity within us. Natural revelation is *God's* activity, not ours. Paul goes on to explain that the knowledge of God that he continually gives us is, because of our sin, continually suppressed by us. We hold it down; we do not want it. In our sin, we will not submit to God or follow him. We refuse to give him honor or thanks (v. 21).

There is more to Paul's discussion that needs to be mentioned. In the last verse of this chapter (v. 32), Paul says, "Although they know God's righteous decree that those who do such things deserve death, they not only continue to do these very things but also approve of those who practice them." Paul is still discussing "general revelation" here. That revelation includes the fact that all people know "God's righteous decree." By that phrase, Paul means (as he will discuss in chapter 2) the "requirements of the law" that are written on the heart of every human being (Rom. 2:15). Our "natural" knowledge of God includes the knowledge of what God requires of us. Those requirements will not be as specific as what we have in Scripture, but they will include what it means to honor God and to give him thanks.

Now we can begin to see a better way to understand the "agreement of the people." We have a biblical interpretation of why it is that a majority of people across the ages have maintained some kind of belief in a god. Paul gives us a twofold reason: (1) Every person knows the true God; each of us carries the truth that God implants in us, including a knowledge of what he requires of us. (2) When we refuse to acknowledge what we know to be true and instead suppress that knowledge, our suppression will include making idols and creating other religions to avoid the truth that God continually gives to us. So, says Paul, our suppression includes an exchange of the truth for "images" (Rom. 1:23). Those images (idols) are the gods we worship and serve (v. 25).

The fact that so many people throughout history have been so religious is not an argument *for* the existence of God. Instead, if we let Scripture interpret the "agreement of the people," we see it as evidence *that* people know God and yet, in their rebellion against that knowledge, refuse to submit to him. In other words, the "agreement of the people" argument is what it is because of the true knowledge of God that all people have. Instead of the "agreement of the people" pointing forward to the conclusion that a god probably exists, it points backward to the knowledge of the true God that all people have (even as we seek to suppress that knowledge), because we are all image of God.

We believe in God because we are human beings. We are image of God, created by the God who continually makes himself known to each and every one of us. In that sense, belief in God is something that always and everywhere, deep within our hearts, is urging itself on us. It is the most natural thing we can do.

"External" Reasons

The reason we have placed quotation marks around "Internal" Reasons and "External" Reasons in this section is because we are making a distinction between two things that actually belong together. God's revelation in and through creation is always and everywhere both "internal" and "external." They are so tightly connected that it is impossible to separate them.

The distinction is helpful in that, as we discussed in the previous section, the "internal" aspect of God's revelation helps us to see the "agreement of the people" argument for what it is. It is a testimony to the fact that all people do (internally) know the true God but, in rebellion, seek to suppress it. That suppression creates idolatry. We will believe in *a* god—an image that we will worship and serve—but we will not acknowledge the true God.

In the same way, when we think of the "external" reasons for believing in God, we are thinking not specifically about what

God is "implanting" (to use Calvin's word) in us, but what God is showing us, externally, through the world that we experience every day.

This too is what Paul has in mind in Romans 1:18–2:23. God is making himself known "from what has been made." He is pointing us to ourselves ("internal"), but also to the world around us ("external"). God's revelation is in all of creation, inside of us and outside of us. That revelation gives a certain strength to some of the so-called "proofs" for God's existence.

For example, one of the more popular arguments for God's existence is the argument from cause and effect (often called "the cosmological argument"). There are variations of this argument, but the substance of it goes something like this: Everything that comes to be has a cause; the universe came to be; therefore, God caused the universe.

An argument like this is patently obvious to any Christian. It has compelling force to Christians because we recognize the biblical truth that it communicates.

But what about someone who is not a Christian? What might an atheist, for example, think about this argument? We don't have to guess at an answer. The famous British atheist Bertrand Russell, in an essay titled "Why I Am Not a Christian," said this about the "First Cause" (cosmological) argument:

> I may say that when I was a young man, and was debating these questions very seriously in my mind, I for a long time accepted the argument of the First Cause, until one day, at the age of eighteen, I read John Stuart Mill's Autobiography, and I there found this sentence: "My father taught me that the question, Who made me? cannot be answered, since it

immediately suggests the further question, Who made God?" That very simple sentence showed me, as I still think, the fallacy in the argument of the First Cause. If everything must have a cause, then God must have a cause. If there can be anything without a cause, it may just as well be the world as God, so that there cannot be any validity in that argument.[10]

Russell recognized that the notion that everything must have a cause included God. If one wanted to argue that God was not caused, why not just believe that the universe was not caused?

In some ways, we can see the problem in Russell's analysis of this argument. We could say to him (something like), "But Lord Russell, don't you see? The very idea of God includes someone who could not be caused by anything. It is not that everything has a cause, but that every effect has a cause. God is no effect." To which Russell would likely reply, "First you tell me that everything that comes to be has a cause, then you tell me God is not caused. I see that you believe that. The problem is, it is that idea of an uncaused God which I do not believe. I am quite happy to have cause and effect in everything. I don't need an uncaused cause."

It should be encouraging to us to recognize that when such arguments are given, they have a very strong appeal. They have an almost overwhelming appeal, because the knowledge of God within us is "connected" to the revelation of God outside of us. The universe had a cause. The cause of all things is God (Gen. 1:1). To say so is to affirm what God himself is revealing in all of creation.

Russell, and all others who are in rebellion against God, work tirelessly to suppress what is obvious in the world. For him, believing in an uncaused universe is all he needs. He doesn't need an uncaused God. He will believe in an uncaused universe not because the "cosmological" argument is bad in itself but because he knows that to agree to the conclusion of the argument would require him to repent, to honor God, and to give him thanks. As a rebel against God, he will twist the argument. If he didn't, it would require him to ask how he can be forgiven by the God he has offended. But his rebellion will run away from such a requirement, and the sin within will push with all its might to avoid admitting such a thing.

Other "external" arguments for belief in God have been pursued. The fact that our existence is limited and dependent means something must exist with unlimited and independent existence. The intricate design of the universe—in its smallest components as well as in the billions of galaxies—requires someone bigger who designed it all. "You wouldn't come across a watch in a desert," so the argument goes, "without recognizing that such a complex and well-designed device must have been designed by an intelligent and skilled person."

All of this "external" evidence of God's existence does indeed testify of his existence. Each and every one of them reveals that God exists and is who he says he is. These are not facts in the world that are simply there for us to interpret as we wish. They are, first and foremost, God's facts as he reveals himself through each one. To point them out as evidence of God's existence is to point to what ought to be obvious to everyone.

But sin clouds, distorts, and hides the obvious. It blinds us, renders us deaf, and makes us like corpses when it comes to the things of God. How, then, can we ask the blind to see, the deaf to hear, and corpses to come to life?

Digging Deeper

When we think of reasons why some do not believe in God, we have to dig below the surface of such beliefs. It will not do simply to tell them that they need an uncaused cause, or a Designer, or one whose existence is necessary. Those statements are true enough, but they don't always get to the heart of the problem.

For example, let's take Russell's objection. Russell says, in effect, "If there needs to be anything without a cause, it may just as well be the world rather than God." If we think carefully about what Russell is saying here, we can get closer to his real reason for rejecting God.

How could it be, we would ask, that if we're looking for an "uncaused cause," the world is as good a candidate as God? Or on what basis can Russell believe that the world is uncaused? How would he go about arguing for that belief?

Russell holds that we should believe only what can be established by evidence. What evidence is there that the world is uncaused? He would find himself in a difficult spot trying to answer that question. Science has not discovered anything that is "uncaused." Everything we know about the world, to the extent that we can know it, depends on other aspects of the world in order to be what it is. Russell could not point to one thing in the world that is not caused by anything at all.

Why think that an uncaused world is as good an answer as an uncaused God? The answer is obvious. Russell has decided that it is better to have faith, a blind faith, that the world is uncaused than to believe that God caused it. There is no evidence that shows the world to be uncaused. But Russell is going to believe it, regardless of its lack of evidence or support. This is the very definition of "blind faith."

The atheist Thomas Nagel, in contrast to Russell, is much more honest about his atheism. Instead of pretending that he is being thoroughly scientific in his atheism, Nagel says,

> I want atheism to be true and am made uneasy by the fact that some of the most intelligent and well-informed people I know are religious believers. It isn't just that I don't believe in God and, naturally, hope that I'm right in my belief. *It's that I hope there is no God! I don't want there to be a God*; I don't want the universe to be like that. My guess is that this cosmic authority problem is not a rare condition and that it is responsible for much of the scientism and reductionism of our time. One of the tendencies it supports is the ludicrous overuse of evolutionary biology to explain everything about human life, including everything about the human mind. . . . This is a somewhat ridiculous situation.[11]

Russell's problem with the cause/effect argument is that he blindly chooses to end the argument with an unsupported belief in an uncaused universe. He does this not because it is more scientific or more rational. He does it because, like Nagel, he does not want there to be a God!

This is what Paul means by suppression of the truth. God caused the universe. Russell knows this because he knows God, and all who deny it know it too. But the knowledge God gives them is continually held down. They will never admit the truth of it until their wills are changed. Instead, they will interpret the words in a way that will produce a "blind faith" conclusion. The problem with Russell, and with any who choose to hold down the truth, is not that the external and internal evidence is insufficient for them to believe in God. The problem, as Nagel says, is that they do not want there to be a God!

Responses

What, then, do we do if the problem is located in what people want rather than in what they think?

In this section, I would like to show how we might respond to people whose hearts are committed to not believing in God. Though the problem remains, at root, a heart problem, the heart is often changed through the mind. Or, to put it another way, one way to challenge the heart is to challenge the mind.

Let's stick to the examples we've already used at the beginning of this chapter. Remember Christoper Hitchens's objection to religion? He complains (in the subtitle of his book) that "religion poisons everything." He is agitated that religion "cannot be content with its own marvelous claims and sublime assurances. It *must* seek to interfere with the lives of nonbelievers, or heretics, or adherents of other faiths."

The natural question that we would want to ask him is this: "What's *wrong* with interfering with others' lives?" Or, more generally, we might ask, "What's wrong with poisoning everything?"

We have to recognize that when we ask this question, we are not asking it of ourselves. We are asking Hitchens, or someone like him, to tell us, according to his own atheistic moral code, why interfering with others, or poisoning the minds of other people, is bad.

To ask this question gets to one of the many deeper problems for those who refuse to believe in God. If there is no God, then how does one determine what is good and what is bad? On what basis does someone like Hitchens accuse Christians of something bad?

It will not do simply to point to something like an "agreement of the people" argument. There was an "agreement of the people" in Nazi Germany. There is an "agreement of the people" among Islamic terrorists. An "agreement of the people" response, when we're looking for a foundation for what is good and what is bad, can "prove" whatever any group of people thinks is proper.

We could also ask Hitchens how a Christian's "interference" with "nonbelievers" is bad, but Hitchens's own interference is apparently proper. Why, for example, is it bad for Christians "not to be content with their own claims and assurances," but it is all right for Hitchens to display such discontent himself. Doesn't writing articles and books promoting and peddling atheism and hatred for all things religious pass beyond the bounds of personal contentment to "interference" with others who don't believe like he does? Doesn't the fact that he traveled all over the world promoting his views betray a basic zeal for *his* view? Like Haman, Hitchens is hung on the gallows he himself built for others (see Est. 7:10). He is trapped by his own words.

The same problem plagues Richard Dawkins. All we need to do is probe a bit more deeply into his own assessment to expose its absurdity. Dawkins thinks the universe displays "pitiless indifference," and he thinks anyone opposed to random evolution is stupid or insane (maybe even wicked).

The question, of course, is why any opposition to evolution is not indifferent. What does it matter, on his own basis, if someone is stupid or insane? Doesn't the fact that he claims evolution to be, by implication, the theory of the intelligent and the rational mean that he thinks it is not indifferent, but it is somehow better (because true?) to believe such a thing? But how can something be "better" (or "true") when all there is are blind, random events combined with utter indifference? Wouldn't this mean that everything that Dawkins believes is itself a product of blind, random events and utterly indifferent? If he really believed that, would he spend so much time and energy trying to convince the rest of us of his views? It seems Haman's pole is getting more and more crowded.

This holds true for any view of the evolution of human beings. Any random process which by itself is said to produce human thoughts and ideas, by definition, means those thoughts and ideas are random events. As many thinkers have shown, all that nature can do is produce more nature. It cannot produce rationality, or morality, or justice, or love, or anything else that makes us truly human.

Conclusion

Not everyone is as strident as the New Atheists. Most people who don't believe in God live every day without outward animosity toward Christianity and without detailed arguments and assertions about their lack of belief. What do we say to such people about our own belief in God?

The good news is that no matter how articulate and educated the denial of God is, the diagnosis is always the same. Remember how Dawkins characterized the "God of the Old Testament"? According to him, this God is, among other adjectives, "the most unpleasant character in all fiction: jealous and proud of it; a petty, unjust, unforgiving control-freak; a vindictive, bloodthirsty ethnic cleanser."

Any Christian reading this description shrinks in horror at such a description. Why be so hateful and vindictive toward God? The answer is concisely stated by Nagel: "It's that I hope there is no God! I don't want there to be a God."

Dawkins, at root, is no different than anyone else who will not believe in God. Their lack of belief is not due to a paucity of evidence—we've already seen that the entirety of creation is clear evidence of God's existence. Nor is it due to not hearing just the right kind of argument. In the end, for Dawkins, Hitchens, and everyone else, the reality is that they "don't want there to be a God."

French philosopher Jean-Paul Sartre was honest about his atheism. He didn't want there to be a God because he knew if there was a God, he could not be free. The problem is in what they want. It is a problem of the rebellious heart.

Our criticisms are meant to show the irrationality of what those who refuse to believe propose. Even if those criticisms succeed, we must not rest content. We must still help people recognize the alternative.

The only thing powerful enough to change the rebellion of the human heart, which itself is enslaved to sin, is the truth of God in the gospel. This is true for those like Dawkins who pretend to have a scientific, or rational, reason not to believe, and for others whose reasons are less detailed or developed. The sinful chains that bind the heart must be broken. Only the gospel can do that.

But as we are concerned to help others understand why we believe, we must do so by appealing to the truth. That truth includes the knowledge of God "inside" that all people have. It also includes the evidence of God "outside" that is universally present, as God is constantly speaking in and through the things he made. More centrally, it includes the fact that we must believe in Jesus Christ and trust him to save us from our sin.

We began this book with that insightful quote from C. S. Lewis: "I believe in Christianity as I believe that the sun has risen: not only because I see it, but because by it I see everything else." This is the point we have to remember when we are attempting to answer the question of why we believe in God and why others ought to believe as well.

It will not do simply to say that we believe in God because of certain evidence because, as we have seen, all evidence is interpreted by people. If those people will not see the evidence for what it is, more must be said. We have to help people understand why, without my belief in God, I can't rightly see anything else in the world. My belief in the Christian God lights up the world, giving me a proper and clear view of it—and of myself as a sinner.

With my belief in God, I do have a standard for what is right and what is wrong. Unlike Hitchens, I can explain why it is wrong to poison everything (though I'll also have to explain why it is sin, not Christianity, that poisons everything). With those like Nagel who believe that their disbelief comes from their will, I can explain how sin has so bound the will to a rejection of God that only something as supernatural and powerful as the good news of the gospel can break its bondage.

To the question, "Why do you believe in God," we can begin to elaborate on what it means through Christ to "see" and make sense of everything. Apart from that belief, there is no "sun" by which to see anything properly. Without our belief in God, we remain blind, deaf, and dead to the glory of God in the world. Only God, in the life-giving gospel, can change that.

Questions for Reflection

1. What do you think is the most compelling argument against God's existence, and why?
2. What do you think is the most compelling argument for God's existence, and why?
3. Explain why your belief in God is not a "blind faith."
4. What is the relationship between your belief in God and your faith in Christ?

Recommended Reading
(from least difficult to more difficult)

Edgar, William. *Reasons of the Heart*. Grand Rapids: Baker, 1996.

Oliphint, K. Scott. *The Battle Belongs to the Lord*. Phillipsburg, NJ: P&R, 2003.

Oliphint, K. Scott. *Covenantal Apologetics: Principles and Practice in Defense of Our Faith*. Wheaton, IL: Crossway, 2013.

Oliphint, K. Scott. *Should You Believe in God? Christian Answers to Hard Questions*. Phillipsburg, NJ: P&R, 2013.

Van Til, Cornelius. *Christian Apologetics*. ed. William Edgar. Phillipsburg, NJ: P&R, 2003.

CHAPTER 3

WHY BELIEVE IN JESUS?

I will never forget taking my family to the "Christmas Spectacular" at Radio City Music Hall one Christmas season. I had heard much about it for years and was delighted that we all had the opportunity to go. It was filled with Christmas songs, including a multitude of dance numbers by the Rockettes, and a special appearance by Santa Claus.

At the end of all the standard Christmas fare, I was shocked when the last scene began. For some reason, I had never heard of this scene, so it came completely unexpectedly. Men dressed as shepherds began to emerge on the stage; others dressed as "wise men" led their camels into the scene. The scene was focused on a man and a woman, both dressed in first-century Middle Eastern garb, looking down onto a manger. A child was in the manger. Every person coming onto the stage merged together to bow down to this child. Then a man with a deep voice narrated the following:

> *He was born in an obscure village*
> *The child of a peasant woman*
> *He grew up in another obscure village*
> *Where he worked in a carpenter shop*

Until he was thirty when public opinion turned against him

He never wrote a book
He never held an office
He never went to college
He never visited a big city
He never traveled more than two hundred miles
From the place where he was born
He did none of the things
Usually associated with greatness
He had no credentials but himself

He was only thirty-three

His friends ran away
One of them denied him
He was turned over to his enemies
And went through the mockery of a trial
He was nailed to a cross between two thieves
While dying, his executioners gambled for his clothing
The only property he had on earth

When he was dead
He was laid in a borrowed grave
Through the pity of a friend

Nineteen centuries have come and gone
And today Jesus is the central figure of the human race
And the leader of mankind's progress
All the armies that have ever marched
All the navies that have ever sailed
All the parliaments that have ever sat

All the kings that ever reigned put together
Have not affected the life of mankind on earth
As powerfully as that one solitary life.[1]

Here, at the end of a secular celebration of Christmas, was an attempt to change the focus. It was meant to move the audience from the myth of Santa Claus to the reality of the "one solitary life" of Jesus Christ.

The way the scene is set up at the end of this show is also striking. As all the people and animals move toward this infant in a manger, they all bow down and worship him.

But why *would* someone worship him? As poetic as the quoted narration is, there is nothing in its contents that would motivate worship. We might be impressed at the influence of this "one solitary life." We might wonder what made him so influential. But the poem says clearly that the one who led this "one solitary life" died and was put in a borrowed grave. And there it ends. Why worship this dead man who influenced so many? Aren't there a number of people who have had significant influence and who have died?

Where Do We Begin?

As with any "journey," the place where we begin is all important. If we want to know how to get somewhere, the first thing we have to recognize is our starting place. We can't get from here to there unless we first know where here is. The same is true if we want to find out how to get to a proper understanding of who Jesus is. We have to recognize, in our quest, where we begin.

In the nineteenth century, a movement developed that was

often called "The Quest for the Historical Jesus." This movement was an attempt to discover and write about the life of Jesus from a purely naturalistic point of view. In other words, the life of Jesus could have nothing supernatural about it. David F. Strauss, to use just one example, wrote *The Life of Jesus*.[2] In this work, he made his starting point clear. He wanted to get to a "historical" understanding of Jesus by rejecting any supernatural elements or stories about him. He considered all supernatural references to Jesus as myth. He wanted to write about a Jesus who was nothing more than a historical, even if influential, person. Strauss wanted to promote a Jesus who lived "one solitary life." No matter how impressive and influential that life might be, it doesn't seem to be worthy of our worship.

The "historical" Jesus was not God. He performed no miracles. Any reference to him that went beyond the natural was deleted from his life. Because Strauss decided he would include nothing but the natural, his only conclusion would have to be a "natural" Jesus, a Jesus who was as "natural" as we are.

The quest for the historical Jesus has a clear starting point: only the natural is real. Anything that purports to be supernatural is a myth. It is a starting point of a journey where the reader has authority over the sacred text instead of the sacred text over the reader. It is no wonder, then, that Strauss's view of Jesus is so inadequate and leaves so many questions unanswered.

As we saw in chapter 1, the "why" questions we are asking can be answered only if we begin with what the Bible says. To "begin with the Bible" means that we accept the Bible for what it says it is—the Word of God. We cannot pick and choose our favorite parts of the Bible and revise its contents as Strauss did. If we think we can pick and choose, then we assume that we are the authority on various Bible teachings or subjects rather than the Bible itself being the authority. If we start with our own assumed authority, rather than the Bible's authority, we wind up with teachings and ideas that have no more authority than our own basic prejudices. Like Strauss, we wind up with a Jesus that *we* constructed, not the Jesus that Scripture reveals to us.

Why believe in Jesus? The Bible gives us the answer. The Jesus we are to believe in must be the Christ of the Bible. The Jesus we create with our own ideas is not the real Jesus. The Bible agrees that Jesus lived "one solitary life" of extraordinary influence. However, influence alone cannot be the reason for the wholesale commitment of our lives to Jesus. We need to know who this Jesus is, and then we will see more clearly why his influence has been so great for more than two thousand years.

The Jesus of the New Testament

The great Princeton theologian B. B. Warfield summarizes the life of Jesus this way: "In simple fact, Jesus' career was not that of an ordinary man: and the dilemma is inevitable that He was either something more than a normal man or something less. We, like His contemporaries—and His contemporaries like us—have only the alternatives: either supernatural or subnormal, either Divine or else `out of His mind.'"[3]

When we approach the Bible for what it says, and not for what we want it to say, Warfield's conclusion is inevitable. Jesus is not merely a good teacher. His claims are much too extraordinary for that. Let's give some examples of what Scripture says.

First, Jesus is both God and man. The apostle John begins his gospel with this magnificent and mysterious truth (John 1:1–3, 14):

In the beginning was the Word, and the Word was with God, and the Word was God. He was with God in the beginning. Through him all things were made; without him nothing was made that has been made. . . . The Word became flesh and made his dwelling among us. We have seen his glory, the glory of the one and only Son, who came from the Father, full of grace and truth.

Anyone who read or heard these words in the first century (AD) would have seen their similarity to the beginning of the Bible. When the apostle John says, "In the beginning," he is echoing the words of Genesis 1:1. Not only does he repeat those words, but he also tells us how this "Word" was related to creation "in the beginning." The "Word" is the one through whom all things were made. As a matter of fact, says John, there is nothing that was not made through him. In other words, in the beginning, the "Word" himself was Creator.

Aside from the Word's involvement in the creation of all things "in the beginning," there are two crucial, though mysterious, truths that Scripture communicates to us in this passage about just exactly who this Word is.

First, the Word is the one who already was in the beginning. This clearly means that the Word was not part of those things that were made in the beginning. When "the beginning" began, he already was. John makes this abundantly clear when he tells us that "the Word was God." If he was, and is, God, then it cannot be possible that he was created.

Not only is this Word *God*, but he is, at the same time, "with God." So there is one who is both God and who is with God. He *is* God, but he is God with a certain distinction. The rest of the

New Testament expands on that distinction. This "Word" who is God and who is with God is none other than the Son of God himself, the second person of the Trinity (we'll discuss the Trinity in chapter 6).

In one sentence, Scripture has given us enough biblical meat to chew on and try to digest for the rest of our lives. In John 1:1, we are introduced to the Creator, through whom all things are made, who is himself God, and as God is also, in some mysterious way, with God. It would be difficult to conceive of a richer and deeper sentence in all of Scripture.

The second crucial and mysterious truth that John tells us is that this Word "became flesh and dwelt among us." There is no question, at this point, who this Word is. John is telling us about Jesus Christ. He is telling us that Jesus Christ is the one who was in the beginning, who created all things, who is, as fully God, with God *and* who took on human flesh in order to live among us. Everything John is telling us in these few verses about Jesus Christ is bathed in the supernatural. There is no possibility of understanding them unless Jesus Christ is the Word, who is both with God and God.

The other three gospels (Matthew, Mark, and Luke) tell us more about the birth of Jesus and about his reasons for coming. They tell us that, from the very beginning, the life of Jesus was supernatural. Matthew, for example, explains the birth of Jesus this way (Matt. 1:18–23):

> This is how the birth of Jesus the Messiah came about: His mother Mary was pledged to be married to Joseph, but before they came together, she was found to be pregnant through the Holy Spirit. Because Joseph her husband was faithful to

the law, and yet did not want to expose her to public disgrace, he had in mind to divorce her quietly.

But after he had considered this, an angel of the Lord appeared to him in a dream and said, "Joseph son of David, do not be afraid to take Mary home as your wife, because what is conceived in her is from the Holy Spirit. She will give birth to a son, and you are to give him the name Jesus, because he will save his people from their sins."

All this took place to fulfill what the Lord had said through the prophet: "The virgin will conceive and give birth to a son, and they will call him Immanuel" (which means "God with us").

Notice that the very conception of Jesus in the womb of his mother was a supernatural event. It was accomplished by the Holy Spirit. Jesus was not conceived in a "natural" way. Instead, the Holy Spirit supernaturally caused Mary to be pregnant.

This Spiritual conception of Christ, in the womb of Mary, was not simply another of many miracles reported in Scripture. It was vital and necessary because of the mission that the Son of God, in the flesh, came to accomplish. As the angel said to Joseph, this child in the womb would be called Jesus. That name, derived originally from the Hebrew name "Joshua," means "Yahweh (i.e., God) is salvation." There were others, of course, who had that name. There are people today who have the name "Jesus."

The name highlights Jesus as the fulfillment of Old Testament expectations. What is important is why Joseph was to call him "Jesus." He is to be called Jesus "for he will save his people from their sins."

This announcement from the angel locates the center of all

of history. It is the reason, for millennia, centuries were labeled either as "BC" (before Christ) or as "AD" (Latin for *anno Domini*, in the year of our Lord). Since the time when sin entered the world (see Gen. 3), the problem of sin is *the* problem of all of humanity. Whatever in the world is bad, or evil, or inhumane, or wicked—all of it is a product of sin. The influence of sin is incalculable in the world. It wreaks havoc on the world, and on every individual in the world. The greatest need of humanity is the destruction of sin.

But no person, until Christ came, was able to destroy sin and its effects. Because every person was a sinner from birth, there was no way to destroy it. Instead, sin's design is to destroy us.

When the angel announced that this Jesus would save his people from their sins, he was announcing that the greatest need that people have would be met in this one who was conceived in Mary's womb. This one, and he alone, could destroy sin and its effects because, unlike everyone else, he was not conceived in sin (see Ps. 51:5). He was conceived in holiness, because he was conceived by the *Holy* Spirit.

We believe in Jesus because he is both the Word of God and God. We believe in him because his birth marks the center of all of history. We believe in him because he took on a human nature so that he could save his people from their sins.

But there is more. Jesus did not hide himself away, attempting to avoid the pollution of the world around him. He did not stay at home with Mary and Joseph until it was time for him to die. Instead, he put himself right in the middle of the people, including the religious people who, because of their knowledge of the Old Testament, should have recognized him for who he was.

In one of his first synagogue appearances, Jesus stood up and read from Isaiah 61 (Luke 4:18–19): "The Spirit of the Lord is on me, because he has anointed me to proclaim good news to the poor. He has sent me to proclaim freedom for the prisoners and recovery of sight for the blind, to set the oppressed free, to proclaim the year of the Lord's favor." Jesus then told those who were in the synagogue that he was the fulfillment of that prophecy from Isaiah. He spoke to them about the way that they, the Jews, had treated the Lord's prophets. This enraged those who heard him and they drove him out of the synagogue and out of town.

On another occasion (see Mark 2:1–12) Jesus was at home. His reputation had grown so much that his home was packed with people wanting to see and hear him. Some men, who had a paralyzed friend, could not get into the home, so they lowered their friend down through the roof. Jesus saw the commitment of this paralytic's friends and he told the paralyzed man that his sins were forgiven.

Two amazing and almost unbelievable things happen after Jesus does this. Some of the religious leaders who are there begin to accuse Jesus silently, in their hearts. They are inwardly outraged at him for saying this man's sins were forgiven. Sin is, ultimately, against God. They rightly recognized that only God could forgive sins.

Mark tells us that Jesus knew what these leaders were thinking in their hearts. This alone shows his divinity. God alone knows the hearts of people (Ps. 44:21; Acts 15:8). So, in order to show them that he has the authority to forgive sins, Jesus does something only God can do: "'But I want you to know that the Son of Man has authority on earth to forgive sins.' So he said to the man, 'I tell you, get up, take your mat and go home.' He got up, took his mat and walked out in full view of them all. This amazed everyone and they praised God, saying, 'We have never seen anything like this!'" (vv. 10–12). The one by whom all things were created, who is now in human form walking the earth, is able, by the same word that created, to speak a word and "re-create" this man's power to walk. Many who were there understood what they had seen, so they "praised God" because of it.

Jesus engaged in a public ministry. He wanted people to know who he was and why he had come. On another occasion (John 8:48–58), Jesus was again confronted by the religious leaders. They were convinced that he was demonic and could not in any way be "one of them." They confronted him with questions about his, and their, identity. Jesus plainly told them that if they would do as he said, they would never die (see v. 51).

The religious leaders interpreted this in light of their own religious tradition. Clearly, Jesus was making himself out to be greater than their father, Abraham, and greater than the prophets.

What follows in this brief discussion contains some of the most remarkable statements ever uttered by Jesus. The Jews were trying to show that there was no way that Jesus could be greater than Abraham. First, Jesus tells them plainly that God is not their Father, since they do not know him (John 8:54–55). When they question how it could be that such a young man like Jesus could know Abraham, Jesus responds: "Very truly I tell you . . . before Abraham was born, I am!" (John 8:58). This statement enrages these leaders and they pick up stones to throw at him.

The reason they are so enraged is because they know—since they are experts in what the Old Testament says—that Jesus has just claimed to be the "I am" who met Moses on the mountain in Exodus 3. In other words, Jesus has just clearly said that he is the very same God that these leaders read about in their Bibles!

Occasions like this are multiplied many times over in the four gospels. We have not even looked at what the rest of the New Testament says about the identity of Jesus. This much, however, is clear: There is no way that the Jesus of the Bible can be "naturally" defined. There is no way that he can be simply a good teacher.

Imagine walking into a church and hearing someone read the portion of Isaiah that Jesus read, and then say to the congregation, "I am the fulfillment of this prophecy!" Or imagine speaking to a large gathering and turning to someone in need and saying to them, "Your sins are forgiven." Or imagine someone saying to you and a group of people you were with, "I am the God who is revealed throughout the Old Testament."

No matter what else this person would say—no matter what "good" he might do—you could not say that this man was a good, moral person. At minimum, you would be extremely worried about his mental state!

Unless, of course, it was all true. If it is all true, then Jesus was not simply "one solitary life" who influenced many people. He is the Lord of heaven and earth, who came down to remove the plague of sin that we perpetuate in our own hearts, and in the world. We believe in Jesus, in other words, because without him, there is no hope for humanity.

The Jesus of the Old Testament

There is another fuller and richer reason why it is crucial for us to believe in Jesus. This reason fills out the reasons that we have just looked at. It is a reason that has too often gone unnoticed. But it is a reason that encompasses the whole of history, not just history since the conception, birth, and life of Christ. It is a reason that begins at the beginning.

In one sense, the Son of God, the second person of the Trinity, reveals God to us from the moment sin entered the world! The great Dutch theologian Herman Bavinck explains it this way:

In a sense *God's becoming human starts already imme-diately after the fall*, inasmuch in his special revelation God reached deeply into the life of the creation, linked up with the work of his own providence, and so ordered and led persons, situations, and events, indeed the entire history of a people, that he gradually came close to the human race and became ever more clearly knowable to it. *But it reaches its culmination only in the person of Christ*, who therefore constitutes the central content of the whole of special revelation. He is the Logos who made and sustains all things (Jn. 1:3; Col. 1:15; Heb. 1:3), and may be considered the angel of YHWH . . . and the content of prophecy . . . ; and in the fullness of time he became flesh and dwelt among us. Thus Christ is the mediator both of creation and re-creation. . . . In creation and in providence . . . , and in the leading of Israel . . . , he prepared his own coming in the flesh. Special revelation in the days of Old Testament is the history of the coming of Christ.[4]

As Bavinck says, God's becoming man starts at the entrance of sin, at the fall of Adam and Eve. This does not mean, of course, that the Son of God takes on a permanent human nature, as he does at the incarnation. What it does mean is that the Son of God is the "Revealer" of God, even at the beginning.

This truth has not received the attention it should. Its truth helps us recognize that the same person who came permanently as the God-man was the one who came temporarily in the Old Testament. Jesus said to the Jews, as we saw in John 8, that he was the one who was on the mountain with Moses in Exodus 3. The one who said to Moses, "I am who I am," in the Old Testament is the same person who came to die for the sins of his people in the New Testament.

Princeton theologian Charles Hodge, in his comments on 1 Corinthians 10:4 ("For they drank from the spiritual rock that accompanied them, and that rock was Christ."), says this about Jesus:

> This passage distinctly asserts not only the preexistence of our Lord, but also that *he was the Jehovah of the Old Testament*. He who appeared to Moses and announced himself as Jehovah, the God of Abraham, who commissioned him to go to Pharaoh, who delivered the people out of Egypt, who appeared on Horeb, who led the people through the wilderness, who dwelt in the temple, who manifested himself to Isaiah, who was to appear personally in the fulness of time, is the person who was born of a virgin, and manifested himself in the flesh. He is called, therefore, in the Old Testament, an angel, the angel of Jehovah, Jehovah, the Supreme Lord, the Mighty God, the Son of God—one whom God sent—one with him, therefore, as to substance, but a distinct person.[5]

As soon as we recognize this wonderful truth, we also begin to read all of redemptive history differently. When God appears in human form in the Old Testament, it is the Son of God appearing in temporary human form in order to show to the Old Testament people what will one day permanently happen in history.

For example, John Calvin, in a discussion of Genesis 32, as Jacob wrestles with the angel, says, "And the confession of the holy patriarch sufficiently declares that he was not a created angel, but one in whom full deity dwelt, when Jacob says, "I have seen God face to face" [v. 30]. Hence, also, that saying of Paul's that Christ was the leader of the people in the wilderness [1 Cor. 10:4]; because even though the time of humbling had not yet arrived, that eternal Word nevertheless set forth a figure of the office to which he had been destined."[6] The "angel" that Jacob wrestled was the "Angel of the Lord," who is the Son of God. This is why Jacob could say that he saw God face to face.

The New Testament has numerous signals that point to the Son in the Old Testament. New Testament writers often take passages referring to Yahweh (or Jehovah) in the Old Testament and, without qualification or explanation, refer them to Christ (see, for example, Rom. 9:33; 14:11; 1 Peter 3:15). Jude tells us explicitly that it was Jesus who brought the people of Israel out of Egypt (v. 5). The apostle John tells us, in John 12:41, that the vision of majesty and holiness that Isaiah saw in the temple (Isa. 6:1–13) was the vision of the glory of the Son of God.

After Jesus rose from the dead, he was walking to the town of Emmaus. Some disciples of Christ were walking to Emmaus, discussing what had happened to their Teacher. When Jesus met them on the road, they were kept from recognizing him. He asked them what they were discussing, and they told him what had been reported about Jesus, but they did not understand why or how such things had happened. So Jesus said to them, "'How foolish you are, and how slow to believe all that the prophets have spoken! Did not the Messiah have to suffer these things and then enter into his glory?' And beginning with Moses and all the Prophets, he explained to them what was said in all the Scriptures concerning himself" (Luke 24:25–27). These disciples were given the best teaching on the interpretation of the Bible ever given!

But notice what Luke says. He says that Christ began "with Moses and all the Prophets," and he helped them understand those passages in "all the Scriptures" (the Old Testament!) as passages that reveal him.

Too often it is thought that the only reason to believe in Jesus is because of what we read in the New Testament. Without a doubt, the New Testament tells us of the climactic and permanent revelation of the Son of God in human form. Only there do we see the conception, birth, growth, life, and death of the God-man.

But all of the history of redemption looks forward to that unique event. The same Son who permanently took on a human nature and came to earth was the one who had been coming to all of the saints ever since sin entered the hearts of people.

What this means for us is that we believe in Jesus, in the first place, because of what he has permanently become, and done, as we read of that in the New Testament. But all that he is and does in the New Testament can be properly understood only in light of who he is and what he does in the Old Testament! In other words, we believe in Jesus because the whole Bible—all of the history of God's redemption of his people—reveals him. The Scripture shows us the central place he has in all of human history.

It should not surprise us, then, that we also believe in Jesus because the end of human history cannot properly be understood without him.

Jesus and the End of History

When Christ finished his earthly work as the God-man, he told his disciples that all authority had been given to him (Matt. 28:18). He was now going to his Father, to reign over the whole earth (see, for example, Heb. 1:1–4). His reign includes the fact that he is building his church (Matt. 28:19–20). But there will be a day when he will return, and he will return to judge all the earth.

When the apostle John was exiled on the isle of Patmos, he experienced something that he never could have imagined. He hears a voice telling him to write what he is about to see. Then, says John,

> I turned around to see the voice that was speaking to me. And when I turned I saw seven golden lampstands, and among the lampstands was someone like a son of man, dressed in a robe reaching down to his feet and with a golden sash around his chest. The hair on his head was white like wool, as white as snow, and his eyes were like blazing fire. His feet were like bronze glowing in a furnace, and his voice was like the sound of rushing waters. In his right hand he held seven stars, and coming out of his mouth was a sharp, double-edged sword. His face was like the sun shining in all its brilliance.
>
> When I saw him, I fell at his feet as though dead. Then he placed his right hand on me and said, "Do not be afraid. I am the First and the Last. I am the Living One; I was dead, and now look, I am alive for ever and ever! And I hold the keys of death and Hades." (Rev. 1:12–18)

The rest of the book of Revelation records the reign of Christ in history. It is a record of Christ's lordship. That lordship is moving toward a specific goal. It is moving toward a day when Christ the Lord will judge every person who has existed. When he comes again, history will be finished:

> He said to me: "It is done. I am the Alpha and the Omega, the Beginning and the End. To the thirsty I will give water without cost from the spring of the water of life. Those who are victorious will inherit all this, and I will be their God and they will be my children. But the cowardly, the unbelieving, the vile, the murderers, the sexually immoral, those who practice magic arts, the idolaters and all liars—they will be consigned to the fiery lake of burning sulfur. This is the second death." (Rev. 21:6–8)

We believe in Jesus because he is the Lord, and we owe our lives to him. When he comes back, the one who knows the hearts of all people will judge each of us. Those who are found to believe in him will be accepted by him because his death covered their sins. Those who refused to believe in him will be punished, eternally, because of their rebellion.

Not only is Jesus the beginning of history; he is the end of history as well. As he says, he is the "Alpha and the Omega." Without him, there is no real hope for our lives on this earth. He is the Lord, and he offers us the privilege of spending an eternity with him. The penalty we deserve has been paid by him for all who believe. Surely, there cannot be a more important reason than that to believe in Jesus Christ:

> "Look, I am coming soon! My reward is with me, and I will give to each person according to what they have done. I am the Alpha and the Omega, the First and the Last, the Beginning and the End.". . . The Spirit and the bride say, "Come!" And let the one who hears say, "Come!" Let the one who is thirsty come; and let the one who wishes take the free gift of the water of life. (Rev. 22:12–13, 17)

Questions for Reflection

1. What is one of the best ways to show someone that Jesus is God?
2. Besides the passages mentioned, what are some other passages in the Old Testament where Jesus appears?
3. Why is it impossible to have real hope unless we believe in Jesus?

Recommended Reading

Gilbert, Greg. *Who Is Jesus?* (9Marks Series) Wheaton, IL: Crossway, 2015.

Sanders, J. Oswald. *The Incomparable Christ*. Moody Classics. Chicago: Moody, 2009.

Sproul, R. C. *Who Is Jesus? Crucial Questions*. Revised, expanded edition. Sanford, FL: Reformation Trust, 2009.

CHAPTER 4

WHY BELIEVE IN MIRACLES?

Reasons

From Hume to Hitchens

How could you believe that an axhead could ever float on water? How could a person walk on water? Can someone really rise from the dead? Questions like these often come to Christians. Embedded in our belief in Christianity is a belief in the reality of miracles. Why would we believe that miracles could happen?

It helps to first consider why the possibility of miracles has been denied. Most objections to miracles will look something like the reasons we will be listing. Also, our responses to the objections should fit in with almost any kind of objection.

The most famous and influential denial of the possibility of miracles is given by the Scottish philosopher David Hume (1711–1776). Hume was a man ahead of his time. In the late eighteenth century, it was still natural for the majority of people to believe in some kind of deity. Eventually, however, and in part because of Hume, belief in some kind of god began to subside. Shortly after Hume died, it became popular to question the existence of anything that was supernatural.

The reason that we need to spend some time laying out Hume's position on miracles is that his argument against miracles has been discussed, re-discussed, and accepted by many since it was written. Hume's argument was so influential that, almost two hundred years later, C. S. Lewis decided to write a book to refute Hume and his many followers.[1] In understanding Hume's argument against miracles, we also understand why many others want to deny miracles, and we can better recognize why we should believe in miracles.

There are sophisticated philosophical ideas and arguments that Hume used to try to refute the notion of miracle. Fortunately for us, there is no need to delve deeply into Hume's philosophy in order to set out and analyze his argument against miracles. Fortunately for us also, looking briefly at Hume's argument will help us to see why we should believe in miracles.

Before we get to Hume, there are a couple of rarely used terms we need to define. The first term is "empiricism"; the second is "probability." To the first, first.

The philosophy that David Hume promoted is called "empiricism." Empiricism simply says that we can know only what we experience. Experiences typically include things that we see, or hear, or touch. For Hume, only those kinds of things are worthy of our beliefs and are able to be known. Because Hume was so insistent that only things of experience could be known by us, his view is sometimes called "naturalism." Naturalism is a view that says only "natural" things can be known. We can know only what we experience, and what we experience is the "natural" world. We can have knowledge of only the natural world; any other kind of knowledge that does not come from the natural world is mere illusion, according to Hume.

In thinking about the possibility of miracles, then, Hume lays out the basic empiricist principle that will guide him: "A wise man . . . proportions his belief to the evidence."[2] This statement defines empiricism. If there is no empirical evidence for a miracle, or if the "proportion" of evidence is only slight, the possibility of miracle has to be rejected.

The second term is "probability." Most of us have some idea of what probability means. In general, it has to do with the likelihood of something happening or taking place. That is how Hume and others use the term. But a likelihood of something always depends on something else. The likelihood, or probability, that I will drive to work depends on what day it is, whether or not I am healthy, whether I own a car, etc. Hence, a probability or likelihood of something happening depends on other things that help determine whether it could happen. With these two terms now before us, we can look at the likelihood of miracles.

In his work titled *An Enquiry Concerning Human Understanding*, Hume ends with a stunning suggestion, a suggestion that gets to the heart of his empirical, "naturalistic" view. He says,

> If we take in our hand any volume; of divinity or school metaphysics, for instance; let us ask, Does it contain any abstract reasoning concerning quantity or number? No. Does it contain any experimental reasoning concerning matter of fact and existence? No. Commit it then to the flames: For it can contain nothing but sophistry and illusion.[3]

Since this is the conclusion to Hume's *Enquiry*, there is a good deal of philosophical argument that precedes it. There is no need to detail that here, though, in order to grasp what Hume is saying.

Hume wants us to picture ourselves in a library. In that library, for example, there are books that deal with Christianity. Take one of the books on Christianity in your hand and open it, says Hume. Now, ask yourself a couple of questions. Does this book on Christianity deal with the science of mathematics? Of course, the answer would be no. Then ask yourself if the book deals with natural things, things that you can experience ("experiential reasoning") in this world. The answer, again, would be no.

Well, says Hume, if the book isn't dealing with the certainties of mathematics (for example, $2 + 2 = 4$), and it is not dealing with things that you see, smell, touch, or hear (for example, trees, flowers, rocks, and birds), then the book has no use. It is better that it be burned than that it be available in a library to lead people astray. Books on Christianity, according to Hume, are "sophistry and illusion." In other words, they deal with only false ideas and fantasies. This is the logical outcome of empiricism.

If this is Hume's view, it should not surprise us that he also argues that miracles cannot happen. Any view that focuses only on the "natural" things of this world will not want to affirm anything that is supernatural.

As we said, Hume's view on miracles has been very influential, but it is also a fairly short argument. The argument that Hume gives assumes that empiricism is true, and that probability is about the best we can expect of our beliefs. So, says Hume, "I flatter myself that I have discovered an argument . . . which, if just, will, with the wise and learned, be an everlasting check to all kinds of superstitious delusion, and consequently, will be useful as long as the world endures."[4] In other words, if books on Christianity should be consigned to the flames because they deal only in illusion, then surely any belief in miracles is likewise a delusion.

Empiricism simply wants to "follow the evidence" and weigh that evidence against other claims that are made. This is the way

Hume will argue against the probability of a miracle happening. We can now state Hume's definition of a miracle, and then show how he proposes to deny any possibility of such a thing:

> A miracle is a violation of the laws of nature; and as a firm and unalterable experience has established these laws, the proof against a miracle, from the very nature of the fact, is as entire as any argument from experience can possibly be imagined.[5]

For Hume, then, a miracle is a "violation of the laws of nature." One of the reasons that Hume's argument has gained so many followers is that his definition seems, at first glance, to be right on target. The world works in a fairly consistent way. It is so consistent that we trust our lives to it. We board an airplane because we recognize (even if we don't fully understand) that the laws of physics are consistent. As the airplane powers itself to a particular speed, the "drag" of the plane is overcome by its propulsion. In other words, when we board an airplane, we trust that if all mechanical systems are working properly, it will fly.

But we also recognize more "mundane" facts. We know that if we place water in a temperature at or below 32 degrees Fahrenheit, it will make ice for us. Our lives are structured around the consistency of the laws that govern our world. Most of these laws are not even things that we think about very much, or that we have to know in any detail in order for them to work. It is sufficient for us to see, or experience, them. The more we see and experience them, the more we trust them. This fact is one reason why empiricism is so tempting for many people.

Hume thinks that the fact that we experience these laws, and the consistency of the world, is enough evidence to prove that miracles cannot happen. He puts it like this: "When anyone tells me, that he saw a dead man restored to life, I immediately consider with myself, whether it be more probable, that this person should either deceive or be deceived, or that the fact, which he relates, should really have happened."[6] In other words, if someone says that he saw someone rise from the dead, we ask ourselves which is more believable, that someone rose from the dead, or that someone has been deceived into thinking such a thing. Which one is more likely, or probable? If it is more probable that someone is deceived than that someone rose from the dead, then "wisdom" requires that we believe that someone is deceived, and *not* that someone rose from the dead. So Hume argues that whenever there is a report of a miracle, we always ask about its likelihood or its probability.

But what is likely is always dependent on other factors. In Hume's thinking, the likelihood of a miracle is always decided based on the likelihood of what is normally or "naturally" the case. Is it more likely that people are sometimes deceived, or that someone rose from the dead? The question answers itself. So, says Hume,

> there is not to be found, in all history, any miracle attested by a sufficient number of men, of such unquestioned good-sense, education, and learning, as to secure us against all delusion in themselves; of such undoubted integrity, as to place them beyond all suspicion of any design to deceive others; of such credit and reputation in the eyes of mankind, as to have a great deal to lose in case of their being detected in any falsehood; and at the same time, attesting facts performed in such a public manner and in so celebrated a part of the world, as to render the detection unavoidable. All which circumstances are requisite to give us a full assurance in the testimony of men.[7]

So, for Hume, the testimony about what is "normal" will always override testimony that something "abnormal," like a miracle, has occurred.

Hume's argument against miracles is thought by many people to be *the* definitive argument. For many who don't believe in miracles, no other argument is needed. Peruse almost any anthology on "the philosophy of religion" and you will find in it Hume's essay against miracles. His argument has a tremendous following, even up to the present day.

For example, the late Christopher Hitchens, an atheist, was completely convinced of Hume's argument. According to Hitchens, "Assuming that a miracle is a *favorable* change in the natural order, the last word on the subject was written by the Scottish philosopher David Hume. . . . A miracle is a disturbance or interruption in the expected and established course of things. . . . If you seem to witness such a thing, there are two possibilities. The first is that the laws of nature have been suspended (in your favor). The second is that you are under a misapprehension, or suffering from a delusion. Thus the likelihood of the second must be weighed against the likelihood of the first."[8] As with Hume, so also with Hitchens. If you weigh the likelihood of a miracle with the likelihood that the person reporting the miracle is under a misapprehension, the second likelihood will win every time. It's beginning to look like there is no possibility that a miracle could occur.

Theism to the Rescue?

But there is a devastating problem with Hume's argument. One of the encouraging things about Hume's argument and influence is that it is fairly easy to detect the problem. Once we see that Hume's argument depends on a certain idea of "nature," we can begin to see its debilitating weakness. C. S. Lewis explains the problem with Hume's notion of "nature": "Now of course we must agree with Hume that if there is absolutely 'uniform experience' against miracles, if in other words they have never happened, why then they never have. Unfortunately we know the experience against them to be uniform only if we know that all the reports of them are false. And we can know all the reports to be false only if we know already that miracles have never occurred. In fact, we are arguing in a circle."[9] This is an ingenious response, and it is perfectly true. The only way Hume can argue against the possibility of miracle is if he sets up the definition of "miracle" so that their possibility is ruled out in the definition itself. Once you assume only the "normal" can be believed, then you define miracle as "abnormal," and there is no possibility of a miracle occurring.

This is a good initial response from Lewis to Hume's argument, but then Lewis makes a fatal misstep. Lewis goes on to say that if we assume the proper understanding of the world, instead of Hume's "naturalistic" understanding, then it is highly probable that miracles could occur. For Lewis, a proper understanding of the world includes the fact that God exists and has created it. Instead of assuming only the "natural," like Hume, why not assume that there is a God and that he created everything? If we begin with that, then, says Lewis, there is an "intrinsic probability" of the "fitness" of miracles.[10] In a theistic universe, the possibility of miracles makes sense.

Is this a sufficient way to respond to Hume and to support our belief in miracles? Do we believe, and should we argue that, given the existence of God, the probability of miracles is very high? Before we propose an answer to that question, it might help to note at least one argument against miracles that includes (unlike Hume) the existence of God.

Before Hume, another philosopher by the name of Benedict de Spinoza (1632–1677) tackled the question of miracles as well. Spinoza, a Jewish theist, asked about the possibility of miracles. His conclusion may be surprising, especially since he moves through certain texts of the Old Testament to his conclusion. As he affirms the existence of God, he also recognizes that the God of the Old Testament is a God who is eternal and unchangeable; he is a God above time who cannot change.

So far, so good. Christianity, too, confesses that God is eternal and unchangeable. But it is exactly this unchangeability that leads Spinoza to conclude that miracles cannot exist. They cannot exist because nature, like the God who made it, must operate according to unchangeable laws. So, says Spinoza, after referring to various texts of the Old Testament, "Now all these texts teach most distinctly that nature preserves a *fixed and unchangeable order*, and that God in all ages, known and unknown, has been the same; further, that the laws of nature are so perfect, that *nothing can be added thereto nor taken therefrom*; and, lastly, that miracles only appear as something new because of man's ignorance."[11] In other words, as we saw with Hume, so we see with Spinoza, the laws of nature cannot allow for any trespasses of those laws. With Hume, the laws of nature *just are*, and any report that they are changed must be because the one reporting is deceived. This is the point that Lewis rightly criticizes.

With Spinoza, however, the laws of nature are given by God in creation. But since they are "laws," and since God cannot change, the laws cannot be violated. If they were to be violated, they would have to be violated by God. Since God is unchangeable, he cannot insert himself into those laws and suspend them or make them operate differently. If he did that, he would have to be subject to change, and God's "laws" would not be laws at all.

It looks like miracles are ruled out if, like Hume, one doesn't believe in God, or if, as with Spinoza, one believes that an unchangeable God exists and that he created the world. Whether a person believes in God or not, it doesn't look like a belief in miracles can be supported. After these philosophers argue that there is no possibility of miracles, do we have any reason to continue to believe in miracles?

Christian Theism to the Rescue

There are two ideas present in the these arguments that need to be understood and corrected. The first idea is that nature is something that moves on its own. With Hume, this idea is obvious. "Naturalists" try to support the notion that nature is all there is. It must, therefore, be "on its own" since there is nothing else. This isn't really argued by Hume, as Lewis points out. He just assumes it and then uses it to conclude that miracles are not possible.

This leads us to the second idea that we need to consider. With Spinoza, the idea of nature is the same as Hume's; nature, even though created, moves on its own. Spinoza recognizes the existence of God, but he also thinks that because God is unchangeable, he cannot interfere with the law-like activity of the world that he has made; if he did, that would require a change in action for God, and a change in the "laws" of nature. So Spinoza thinks that God, because of his character, is unable to interact with, or interfere in, the universe that he made.

If we take these two ideas at face value, it looks like neither theism nor atheism is sufficient for believing in miracles. Fortunately, the weaknesses in the arguments and ideas of Hume and Spinoza are not difficult to see. We have little reason to take these arguments at face value.

As Lewis says, Hume is simply arguing in a circle. He begins with a definition that he does not argue for, and then uses that definition to conclude that there can be no miracles. If you begin by insisting that there can be no miracles, anything else you say will obviously agree with that assumption.

For Spinoza, even though he affirms God as Creator, he still thinks the "laws" of nature move on their own and are not to be violated. He thinks that if God violated them, it would require him, and the laws, to change. And a "changing" God is not what Scripture teaches.

Let's think first about the idea that "nature" moves on its own. This is a standard way to think about the world. Even Christians might be lulled into thinking that God simply set the universe in motion and then left it to itself to do its work.

But Christianity knows nothing of a universe that moves on its own. Consider, for example, the way the psalmist describes the world: "He makes springs pour water into the ravines; it flows between the mountains. They give water to all the beasts of the field; the wild donkeys quench their thirst. The birds of the sky nest by the waters; they sing among the branches. He waters the mountains from his upper chambers; the land is satisfied by the fruit of his work" (Ps. 104:10–13).

The Bible never hesitates to affirm that the workings of nature are the workings of the God who created it all. The earth is satisfied, says the psalmist, *not* simply with the rain, or the birds who sing, but "by the fruit of his work." Spinoza, whose focus on Scripture was only on the Old Testament, should have seen this. The "laws" of nature are actually the faithful activity of a faithful God. After the flood, his faithfulness is shown in the coming and going of the seasons (Gen. 8:22). So when people recognize the change of seasons, that change is not due to some impersonal "law," but it is due to God's faithful and reliable working in the world.

Hume denied miracles because he defined nature as a predictable, closed system. Spinoza denied miracles because he defined nature as invariably law-like. In both definitions, nature is improperly defined. Once we see that nature is what it is because God is working in and through it, it will be no stretch to recognize that the same God who is faithfully giving us seasons can also, if he sees fit, work things differently in order to accomplish his sovereign purposes in creation.

Why would God want to act differently in the world? What would his reasons be for changing his standard, "law-like" way of working in the world?

The answer to this question helps us to see the true meaning of miracles. It is often thought that miracles are just grand "magic tricks." Like a wizard who can wave a wand, God is sometimes thought to be someone who wants to show off his power.

Miracles are not arbitrary displays of God's power. They are given in order to point to the redemption that God accomplishes in Jesus Christ. In other words, miracles are not a collection of magic tricks that God performs. Instead, they are testimonies or acts that point to the fact of God's redemption.

One example of this might help make the point. In Mark 4:35–41 (also Matt. 8:23–27 and Luke 8:22–25), Jesus speaks to the stormy wind and the seas and they become calm. This is a miracle that only the One who created the world could perform. But he doesn't perform this miracle in order to impress his disciples. This is not wizardry or magic. Instead, it was supposed to increase the disciples' faith so that they would trust in him.

Jesus had been talking to his disciples about the kingdom of

God. The calming of the storm was meant to point to him as the King of the kingdom. Jesus performed a miraculous act so that they might better understand his words to them. The act supported the words. This is the main point of the miracles of the Bible. They are acts to support God's words.

When the disciples saw Jesus calm the storm, they should have immediately recognized that he did so to demonstrate that he is the Lord. They should have thought of Psalm 107: "He stilled the storm to a whisper; the waves of the sea were hushed. They were glad when it grew calm, and he guided them to their desired haven. Let them give thanks to the Lord for his unfailing love and his wonderful deeds for mankind" (Ps. 107:29–31). The disciples should have seen the miracle of Jesus calming the storm as a testimony that Jesus himself was the Lord, the same Lord who is spoken of in this psalm. The calming of the storm was meant to be an identity marker of Jesus. Its intent was to say, loudly and with clarity, "This is the Lord of the universe who has come to redeem you! This is the King of the kingdom!"

Instead of believing and being strengthened in their faith, what did the disciples say, "They were terrified and asked each other, 'Who is this? Even the wind and the waves obey him!'" (Mark 4:41). But they should have known who he was. Their own Scriptures identified him, and the miracle was given to them to increase their faith. It was a sign pointing to God's redemptive purposes.

Once we recognize that miracles have a redemptive purpose, we begin to "read" God's *acts* in light of what God *says* in the context of those miracles. The manna that God miraculously provided to his children in the wilderness, for example, was meant to point to the true Bread that would bring eternal life (see John

6:47–51). The raising of Lazarus pointed to the fact that the One who could raise Lazarus from the dead was himself the true resurrection and the life (John 11:25–27).

Whenever you come across a miracle in the Bible, ask yourself, "What redemptive truth is God communicating through this miracle?" Christians believe in miracles because they believe that God is our Redeemer. What he *says* he will do, he also shows he will do through his miracles. When you read the miracles in Scripture with that question in mind, they take on an entirely new, and gloriously redemptive, meaning.

Responses

A couple of objections to our discussion of miracles might come to mind. "OK," someone might say, "you accuse Hume of reasoning in a circle because he starts with the uniformity of nature and so rules out the possibility of miracle at the beginning. Aren't you just reasoning in a circle when you start with God and so include the possibility of miracles at the beginning?"

Here is the main difference between why we believe in miracles and why Hume didn't. When Hume started with "nature" as a closed, law-like uniformity, he had no reason to assume its uniformity. Remember, Hume was an empiricist; only what one experienced could be known. Hume could affirm only what his senses would allow. But Hume had not seen all of "nature," nor had anyone else. He had no experience of it as an entire system. The best he had was his own experiences of nature, or the reports of others. To reason that there could be no miracles at all based on his (or anyone's) limited experience of the world was nothing but speculation.

We believe in miracles because we believe in the triune God. Unlike Hume, our belief in God is not grounded in our experiences. Instead, our belief in God is grounded in what he has said and done. As we noted in chapter 1, the question of "why" will inevitably return to what God has said in Scripture. Unlike Hume, we begin with God, not because we "sense" him, but because he has spoken, and when we trust Christ, we trust what he has said. We do not believe that we can know only what we experience. We believe that we can know because of who God is and what he has done.

"Well," the objector might respond, "what about Spinoza? He believed in an unchangeable God, just like you do, and because of that he could not believe in miracles. How can an unchangeable God act in his world without changing?"

This question is actually one of the deepest questions that can be posed to Christians. But we have already seen that, because God is three persons in one God, he is able, in the person of his Son, to come to this world by taking on a human nature, even while he remains fully and completely God. So, even though we cannot comprehend how God can do this "Grand Miracle" (as C. S. Lewis calls it), that he does it is without question, and it is the center of all that we believe as Christians. Spinoza didn't read the Scriptures properly. If he had, he would have seen that the story of the Bible is the story of God acting in history to save a sinful people. So, we could think of it this way: All the miracles in the Bible are meant to point to, explain, and testify to that great and glorious "Grand Miracle" of God coming to man by becoming man. All other miracles serve that one redemptive act of God.

Conclusion

We believe in miracles because we believe in Christ. When we believe in Christ, we believe that he is the greatest miracle of all. When we believe in Christ we believe what he tells us. What he tells us is that the miracles of the Bible all point to him. Once we believe in him, it is no step at all to believe in those great acts of God that show us his plan of redemption, in and through his Son.

Questions for Reflection

1. What is the difference between a miracle and a magic trick?
2. Does God ever use things he has created in the world to perform a miracle?
3. Why are some miracles in the Bible harmful to people (for example, Exodus 14:27–29. Hint: Exodus 14:31)?

Recommended Reading

Lennox, John. *Miracles: Is Belief in the Supernatural Irrational?* Veritalks, vol. 2. Cambridge, MA: Veritas Forum, 2013.

Lewis, C. S. *Miracles, a Preliminary Study.* New York: Simon and Schuster, 1947.

Metaxas, Eric. *Miracles: What They Are, Why They Happen, and How They Can Change Your Life.* New York: Dutton, 2014.

Warfield, Benjamin Breckinridge. *Miracles Yesterday and Today, True and False.* Grand Rapids: Eerdmans, 1953.

CHAPTER 5

WHY BELIEVE JESUS ROSE FROM THE DEAD?

Reasons

Historical Reasons

On July 21, 1969, Neil Armstrong took "one small step for man, one giant leap for mankind." The first man had stepped on the moon. I was at work that evening and took a break to watch the event on television. It was the second time in my young life (the first being John F. Kennedy's assassination) that I clearly knew I was watching a significant moment in history.

Or was I? It didn't take long before books and articles began to be written about the moonwalk "hoax." In 1974, just five years after the event, Bill Kaysing published *We Never Went to the Moon: America's Thirty Billion Dollar Swindle*. In that book, he argued that the probability for a moon landing was exceedingly low. NASA could have more easily faked a landing than accomplished one.

Suppose you set out to investigate the first moon landing, and all the people involved in that event were now dead. What would you do? How would you go about proving that these men set foot on the moon in 1969?

You would surely begin by taking advantage of the reams of information now available online. You would begin to read original news articles, transcripts of interviews, reports from the astronauts who were there, etc. You would gather all the information you could in order to compile a compelling case for the first moonwalk.

Along the way, as you went through your research, you would also find out that those who think the moonwalk was a fraud had themselves done all of the research that you had done. They had read the news articles, transcripts of interviews, reports from the astronauts, etc. With all of that information, they concluded that the event was a fake; there was no way that it really happened.

How can it be that people can have the exact same information in hand and, with that information, come to opposite conclusions? There are at least two reasons for this.

The first reason has to do with the nature of historical investigation. The problem is not with historical investigation itself. Historical research is a very good thing and is a necessary part of what we all believe and understand about our world. We all believe that Caesar crossed the Rubicon in 49 BC, and with that the Roman Empire began. One of our primary sources for this belief, however, is Suetonius, who wrote more than a century after Caesar's crossing. The earliest manuscript, just one, available of Suetonius is from almost a thousand years after his death. There is a minuscule amount of manuscript evidence available for the life of Caesar.

The point, however, is not to cast doubt on Caesar's crossing of the Rubicon in 49 BC or to call into question the details of his life that are given by Suetonius, Pliny, and other historians. The point is to recognize that historical investigation serves a particular purpose. Its purpose is not to give us absolute certainty regarding what it reports. Instead, historical research and investigation can often give us enough credibility to believe its conclusions.

In Josh McDowell's classic work *Evidence That Demands a Verdict*, he includes an extensive chapter on the credibility of the resurrection. In that chapter, titled "Resurrection—Hoax or History?" McDowell includes quotations from biblical passages and from historians, lawyers, theologians—both ancient and modern—psychologists, former atheists, and others, all giving testimony to the historical truth of the resurrection. These sources can be read with profit. It is an impressive array of testimonials that support the reality of the resurrection in history. At the conclusion of the chapter, McDowell says this, "The decision is now yours to make; the evidence speaks for itself. It says very clearly, 'Christ is risen indeed.'"[1]

John Warwick Montgomery, who is, like McDowell, an apologist for the Christian faith, gives a more honest appraisal in his assessment of the evidence for the claims of Christ, including the resurrection. Montgomery concludes his historical analysis with this: "It should now be very evident to the reader that the possibility of future evidence arising to negate the force of the now existing evidence for Christ's claims is *almost too small* to be entertained, the evidence for the Resurrection involves only four documents, whose dates of origin have been determined beyond a shadow of a doubt. The only relevant *new evidence* which would be pertinent to this problem would seem to be a discovery of Christ's remains . . . , but the possibility of such data ever existing is *virtually* nil."[2]

Montgomery's conclusion helps to explain the nature of historical investigation. Even though sometimes necessary and useful, historical evidence can provide only a probable conclusion. This is why Montgomery has to admit that "the possibility" of future evidence arising that denies Christ's claims is "almost too small to be entertained." We could put this another way and say that, as a matter of fact, this future evidence could be entertained; it could be entertained by anyone who wants to consider it. The probability might be low by Montgomery's standards, but it is still probable. This is why Montgomery has to admit that the possibility of someone discovering Christ's body is "virtually nil." Notice, the possibility of discovering Christ's body is not nil, but virtually nil.

We have to reiterate again that the problem here is not with historical investigation itself. This is the best historical investigation can do, and, as we have said, such investigation is sometimes necessary and useful in a vast amount of areas, not the least of which is in a study of the historical events that are recorded in the Old and New Testaments. Christianity is a historical religion. It did not begin in a hidden corner or with one man receiving a revelation for everyone else. Christianity began in history, and its history should never be ignored or undervalued.

But historical investigation, as Montgomery indicates, can conclude with only some kind of probability. Maybe, after an ample amount of historical research, the probability is high that a certain event happened. But because there remains some probability that the event might not have happened, there's always some level of doubt. It is that kind of doubt that allows for theories of a moonwalk hoax, or of 9/11 attacks being carried out by the United States instead of by terrorists, or of any number of conspiracy theories that abound. These theories may lack plausibility for most people, but what they do not lack is probability, even if the probability is "virtually nil."

So, one could peruse books like McDowell's and Montgomery's. Both books have different ways of presenting the historical evidence of Christianity in general, and of the resurrection in particular. It could be that some will be convinced by that evidence that Christianity is a fact, and even that the resurrection is a fact. "Facts are stubborn things," said John Adams, and sometimes their stubbornness implants itself in our belief system. That is a good thing.

This brings us to the second reason why people can come to opposite conclusions about historical facts. There are things even more stubborn than facts. Those things are our predispositions and biases, our most basic commitments (we will look at an example of this under "Response"). We all have basic commitments that force us to interpret facts in a certain way. The strong disagreements in the culture wars are not primarily over the facts but the interpretation of those facts. The facts of fetal development, for example, are clear; with all of our advances in science, that development can now be viewed at every step. But how we "see" those facts depends on our basic commitments about what we think "life" is, or what we think a "human being" is, etc. In the abortion debate, the facts are the same for all. But it is the basic commitments that make those stubborn facts say different things.

When McDowell says that "the evidence speaks for itself," and that it is "very clear," he is speaking as one who is already committed to Christ. A person who is not thus committed could easily amass a number of authorities and quotations against the resurrection, which evidence would, then, "speak for itself" and would be "very clear" to any who wish to oppose the resurrection of Christ.

Facts are indeed stubborn things, but their stubbornness cannot compare to the almost intractable stubbornness of our baseline commitments. Those commitments become the grid through which we read the facts. Much more than stubborn facts are needed when it comes to our understanding of ourselves, the world around us, and everything else.

Christian Reasons

If all we have are historical reasons for our belief in the resurrection, then it is possible to conclude, with a certain amount of probability, that the resurrection of Jesus Christ happened in history. This is not a bad thing; it can be very useful as we think about the resurrection. It lends a certain amount of credibility to the historicity of Christianity. Of all religions, Christianity is the one that has the most historical evidence, and therefore the least to hide, in what it purports. We should never hide from, or routinely dismiss, the historical aspect of Christianity.

However, we also recognize that, when we are thinking about the "why" question as it pertains to the resurrection of Christ, Christians should never be content to begin and end their belief in the resurrection of Christ with only historical data. Those data can support our belief in the resurrection. They can supplement what we believe and why we believe it. But historical data cannot be the center of our response to the "why" question. If the historical data are at the center, then the best we can say is, like Montgomery, that we believe the resurrection probably occurred. But that will not do; we do not believe in the probability of the resurrection. Instead, the center of our response to the "why" question of the resurrection is that, without the resurrection of Christ, there is, in fact, no Christianity at all.

The reason for this is because the meaning of the resurrection must be tethered to its factual, historical occurrence. Suppose, for example, that someone comes to believe that the resurrection of Christ happened in history. Since our precommitments and prejudices interpret such things, we might want to ask why someone believes such an apparently impossible event. Maybe the response would be, as the Queen of Hearts said to Alice, "Why, sometimes I've believed as many as six impossible things before breakfast."[3] Belief in the resurrection would simply be a belief in something impossible, and nothing more.

The fact of the resurrection of Christ can easily be incorporated into a view of the world that thinks random chance is ultimate. If the universe is running according to the progression of random events, then a resurrection is just one of the "six impossible things before breakfast." After all, strange things happen in a random world. The resurrection takes its place alongside Stonehenge. It is equivalent to the strange notion, suggested by Francis Crick, Nobel Prize winner and discoverer of DNA, that aliens might be responsible for life on Planet Earth.[4] Strange things happen, and it just might be that some other civilization came to earth and began life here.

The reason that Christians believe in the resurrection of Christ, however, is not simply because we believe in miracles or in life after death. The reason that Christians believe in the resurrection is because, since sin came into the world, the fact of Christ's resurrection, together with its meaning, comprises the center of God's entire plan for the world.

The apostle Paul wrote his first letter to the Corinthians around the middle of the first century, some twenty-five years or so after Christ ascended. At the end of this letter, he describes for the church the centrality and significance of Christ's resurrection. His description has little to do with the miraculous character of the resurrection, although it certainly was miraculous. Instead, Paul writes to the church that the resurrection is the central "key" that unlocks the whole of Christianity. There are three aspects to the resurrection that make it central to Christianity, each of which, taken together, answer the "why" question.

The first aspect that Paul mentions is this: "For what I received I passed on to you as of first importance: that Christ died for our sins according to the Scriptures, that he was buried, that he was raised on the third day according to the Scriptures" (1 Cor. 15:3–4). Paul is reminding the church of his ministry among them. In that ministry, Paul is reminding them of the most important part of his ministry to them, and, therefore, of the Christian faith. What is of "first importance" is that Christ died for our sins, was buried, and that he was raised on the third day. Any Christian will readily see that this is the gospel. The good news of the gospel of Jesus Christ is summed up in this one passage.

But notice one crucial aspect to this good news. Paul repeats it two times in order to highlight its source. The death, burial, and resurrection of Christ were all according to the Scriptures. We might be tempted to think that Paul is referring here to the New Testament Scriptures. But that cannot be the case, since much of the New Testament, including the Gospels, has yet to be written as Paul writes this letter. When Paul says he delivered this gospel according to the Scriptures, he is telling them that the gospel he delivered to them has its source in the Old Testament!

Paul is not alone in his affirmation that the work of Christ was given in the Old Testament. After Jesus was raised, he told his disciples the same thing: "He said to them, 'This is what I told you while I was still with you: Everything must be fulfilled that is written about me in the Law of Moses, the Prophets and the Psalms.' Then he opened their minds so they could understand the Scriptures. He told them, 'This is what is written: The Messiah will suffer and rise from the dead on the third day'" (Luke 24:44–46; see also John 20:9, Acts 26:23). The Lord himself testifies that the Old Testament, if properly read, refers again and again—in the Law, the Prophets, and the Psalms—to the fact that Christ will die and rise again.

On one occasion, Jesus rebuked the Pharisees because they were clamoring for a "sign" that would point them to his true identity. Jesus tells them that their request is evil and that they already have a sign, which was given to them in the Prophets: "He answered, 'A wicked and adulterous generation asks for a sign! But none will be given it except the sign of the prophet Jonah. For as Jonah was three days and three nights in the belly of a huge fish, so the Son of Man will be three days and three nights in the heart of the earth'" (Matt. 12:39–40). Their very request for a sign illustrates their lack of understanding of the Old Testament.

Another example of this is given in Paul's address in the synagogue in Antioch. Paul reasons with those who were there that day on the basis of what the Old Testament says about Christ and his work. He tells them, for example, that Psalm 16:10 refers to Christ's resurrection: "'So it is also stated elsewhere: "You will not let your Holy One see decay." Now when David had served God's purpose in his own generation, he fell asleep; he was buried with his ancestors and his body decayed. But the one whom God raised from the dead did not see decay'" (Acts 13:35–37).

Those who knew their Bibles (Old Testament) should have seen that David's statement that God's "Holy One" will not see decay could not refer to David. David was dead and his body had decayed. They should have seen that it would refer to a "Holy One" who would die but not suffer the bodily decay of death, so that he would live again! Christ himself, as well as the apostles, after the resurrection, took their Bibles, which consisted only of the Old Testament, and showed people how the entire Old Testament foretold and looked forward to the work of Christ, which culminates in his resurrection.

The resurrection is more than miraculous (which, of course, it is). It is the golden thread that wraps around and bundles together the entirety of redemptive history. Ever since Adam brought death into the world, the plan of God has been to destroy death through life after death.

The second reason that Paul gives for the centrality of the resurrection is just as comprehensive as the first reason, though instead of comprehending history, it comprehends the entirety of biblical faith. "And if Christ has not been raised, our preaching is useless and so is your faith. More than that, we are then found to be false witnesses about God, for we have testified about God that he raised Christ from the dead. But he did not raise him if in fact the dead are not raised" (1 Cor. 15:14–15). This is a stunning admission. If Christ's resurrection did not happen, then preaching, and the faith that follows it, are all in vain. If there is no resurrection, then "we are of all people most to be pitied" (1 Cor. 15:19) because we are basing our entire lives on a futile and meaningless lie.

The stinging consequence of the sin that Adam brought on himself and on all humanity is death. It is a corruption of that which God gave to Adam and Eve when he made them in his image. He breathed into them the breath of life. Sin kills that life (though it does not kill our eternal existence), but God is determined to make life continue. It can only continue if sin is overcome, that is, if death can be defeated.

But how can sin be overcome? It cannot be overcome by sin, but it has to be overcome by one who is not subject to sin. If there is someone who is not subject to sin, then sin does not overcome him, even though it continues to reign over those who sin. Sin has to be overcome by one who is sinless and who takes sin's penalty on himself. Because of Adam and his progeny, therefore, there must be one who is sinless, and who experiences death, but conquers it by living again, so that life might continue in spite of the death that sin requires.

This is why our faith, which unites us to Christ, is futile, meaningless, and vain if there is no resurrection. The resurrection of Christ is the only way that faith can be living and not futile faith. The dead cannot save the living. To trust in one who is dead (which is the predicament of virtually every other religion) is to render that trust empty and without hope.

To put it in terms of our first and second reasons, if Christ has not been raised, then all that the Old Testament indicates, all that the New Testament declares, all that we gladly admit and assent to—every single bit of Christian truth—is utterly meaningless and without content. It is, in its essence, dead.

The third reason why we believe in the resurrection is connected to the other two. Twice in 1 Corinthians 15, in verses 20 and 23, Paul describes Christ's resurrection as the "firstfruits." This term refers to the practice in the Old Testament of bringing the firstfruits as sacrifices to God (Ex. 23:19). The reason for bringing the firstfruits was not because only the firstfruits belonged to God.

Instead, it was a sacrifice that was meant to confess that the entire harvest belongs to God and is of his own making! Bringing the firstfruits as a sacrifice to God was Israel's way of saying, "Lord, all that I have belongs to you; not simply these firstfruits, but all that you have given." The firstfruits were an offering given that declared that the entire harvest was God's.

The Bible teaches that the resurrection of Christ is the beginning of one single "harvest" event. That event is the resurrection of all who have life in Christ because they have faith in Christ. Faith gives us "a new life" (Rom. 6:4). In other words, the resurrection of those who are in Christ begins when we are in Christ. It is not something that has to wait until we receive our new bodies on the last day. Our resurrection reaches its climax when we receive those bodies, but our new bodies are the completion of what began when we were, by faith, raised in and by Christ himself.

This is why our faith would be in vain without the resurrection. Our faith inaugurates and establishes our resurrection. But if Christ has not been raised, then neither can we have a new life. Without the resurrection, sin remains the principle of death in us. It reigns in us. If that is true, then we should "'eat and drink, for tomorrow we die'" (1 Cor. 15:32).

This last point brings us to consider life after death. In our consideration of the resurrection of Christ, we come to the central reason—and main focus—of why we believe in life after death (more on this in chapter 7).

The principle of life is not one that remains in us intrinsically. It is true that since people are made in the image of God, they will continue to exist for eternity. In that sense, never-ending existence is tied to what it means to be in the image of God.

In the Bible, however, the notions of "life" and "death," while they assume the never-ending existence of each and every person, are much richer concepts than "mere existence." Since the entrance of sin in the world, the notion of "death" is not tied, in the first place, to the end of our earthly existence. "Death" in the Bible means an existence without fellowship and communion with God. When Adam sinned, he and Eve were driven from the Garden, which was the place where life had been promised (Gen. 3:22). The tree of life was closed off to them, and they began their mortal existence barred from the life that they had been offered.

In Revelation 20:6, John writes of a "second death": "Blessed and holy are those who share in the first resurrection. The second death has no power over them, but they will be priests of God and of Christ and will reign with him for a thousand years." The ones who "share in the first resurrection" are the ones who are included in the "firstfruits" of Christ's resurrection. They are the ones who have life. They have life because of the life of Christ in his resurrection.

The resurrection life of Christ is the life that has remained sinless, died, and risen again, and so it is not subject to the effects of sin. Even though Christ was sinless, the resurrection life of Christ is the life that conquered death *by dying*! The death that conquered death was not a death deserved. It was the only death that was not deserved. Instead, it was a death donned, a death taken, a death accepted, so that those who deserve it would not, in Christ, have to endure it for eternity.

Life, in Scripture, is not merely never-ending existence. It is existence in the One who is life because he sinlessly conquered death. All in him will live for eternity. Those who are found to be against him will be consigned to the "second death," which is the eternal lake of fire (see Rev. 20:14; 21:8).

Christians believe in life after death because Christ is risen.

He is not probably risen or probably alive. If he is probably risen, then our faith is probably in vain. But he is risen, and because he lives, we will live. The rest, who exist in opposition to him and his life, will exist eternally in the "second death."

The certainty of the resurrection of Christ gives us the certainty that those in him will live. Any other reasons for believing in Christ's resurrection, other than those given to us in Scripture, can never establish the bedrock truth that Christ is alive, nor can they give us lasting confidence that because he lives, we will live also.

Responses

Objections to the resurrection of Christ are legion. Even from the time of Christ's resurrection, stories were being invented to counter it (see Matt. 28:13). The vast majority of objections have to do with the "historical" problem we mentioned. That problem, as we said, has more to do with a person's basic commitments than it does with the "facts." Other objections have to do with the "problem" of miracles, more generally, and we looked at that in chapter 4.

Instead of repeating what we have said with regard to the "historical" objections and objections about miracles, it might be useful for us, briefly, to look at a couple more specific objections to the resurrection that surface on occasion. These objections will give weight to our previous discussion, especially with regard to "basic commitments."

In his book *The Case Against Christianity*, Michael Martin devotes a chapter to an analysis of the resurrection of Christ. As an atheist, Martin employs some of the standard atheistic objections to the resurrection. We cannot detail them all here. It may be helpful, however, to notice the initial reasons for his skepticism.

Under the heading "Initial Obstacles to Belief in the Resurrection," Martin begins by acknowledging that the Bible recognizes that the resurrection of Christ is a miracle. But, says Martin, "This assumption immediately raises obstacles to its acceptance. First, the believer in Jesus' alleged resurrection must give reasons to suppose that it can probably not be explained by any unknown laws of nature. Since presumably not all laws have been discovered, this seems difficult to do. The advocates of Jesus' resurrection must argue that it is probable that Jesus being restored to life will not be explained by future science utilizing heretofore undiscovered laws of nature."[5] Whenever objections like this are presented, it is often helpful to pause for a minute and notice exactly what is being said.

Notice, first, that Martin imposes an obligation on those who believe in the resurrection. He has decided what believers in the resurrection "must" do. That in itself deserves a question or two. What is the force of the "must" in this statement? Must we give reasons because, without the reasons specified by Martin, our belief is false? That would be impossible to argue. Must we give reasons because, without the reasons specified by Martin, Martin himself can't accept it? More on that in a minute.

But then we notice that the reasons that we must give relate to the probability of the resurrection in light of unknown laws of nature. The absurdity of this requirement should be obvious. If we were to concede Martin's point and agree to his imposed obligation on us, our concession would go something like this: "You know, Michael, you're right. I hadn't considered that my belief in the resurrection of Christ was so improbable against the background of laws of nature that I do not know about. How could I have missed this?"

In other words, Martin's objection to the resurrection is that scientists might, in the future, discover laws of nature that can explain the resurrection. Given that such a thing might happen, we're supposed to demonstrate to him how we can continue to believe in the resurrection.

Let's say, to use an analogy, that I believe I was asleep for six hours last night. I suspect that many others believe that they too were sleeping last night. I have no documentation for such a belief, no pictures or testimonies. Is it irrational for me to believe that I was asleep because scientists might discover, in the future, a previously unknown law of nature that proves that humans never really sleep? Of course not. It is not possible to measure what is rational or irrational based on an unknown future discovery.

The second objection we will mention from Martin is that, since the writers of Scripture were biased in their reporting of the resurrection, that reporting should not be believed. Here's what he says: "Alleged miracles may be due not to some trick or fraud but to misperception based on religious bias. *A person full of religious zeal may see what he or she wants to see, not what is really there.* We know from empirical studies that people's beliefs and prejudices influence what they perceive and report. The question therefore arises, was Jesus restored to life and did he appear to his disciples or was his body stolen and did his disciples 'see' what they wanted to see?"[6]

What may seem obvious on a first read of this objection, for some reason, is not so obvious to Martin. When Martin says, "A person full of religious zeal may see what he or she wants to see, not what is really there," he doesn't recognize that such a statement applies equally to him. Perhaps he thinks his atheism is significantly different from a "religious zeal." But it isn't.

Since our biases affect how we see things, the biases of the gospel writers are no more a threat to the fact of the resurrection than are Martin's biases against it. In each case, there is strong bias, and those biases move us to believe certain things in certain ways. Since Martin approaches the subject of Christ's resurrection as an atheist, it is no surprise that he is going to "see" the resurrection in a certain way.

This is why the reasons we might give for our belief in the resurrection, if given according to Martin's own terms, would never be acceptable to him. His atheistic bias both establishes the ground rules for proper belief in the resurrection and the conclusions as to whether those rules are properly applied.

We can begin to see why Martin wants to require that believers in the resurrection justify their belief on the basis of unknown, future scientific laws. It is the strong "religious" atheistic bias and zeal of Martin that produces such an incoherent test for our belief in the resurrection. Bias can indeed render one blind to the obvious.

Instead of conceding to Martin's demands, a more profitable discussion might begin by giving account of our own respective biases, and then asking how far those biases and prejudices can take us in understanding the world and ourselves in the world. The resurrection, though central to the gospel and to Christianity, can be what it is only within the context of an entire Christian worldview. Within any other worldview, it is simply a strange occurrence.

There is more that we could say about Martin's objections, but this should suffice for now. For anyone interested, a perusal of the rest of Martin's "case" against Christianity might actually help Christians recognize just how firm their belief is, especially when seen against the background of Martin's atheism.

Conclusion

Is the resurrection of Christ a hoax or is it a historical fact? How much weight can we give to the evidence? Michael Martin thinks that clear and empirical evidence must be given. What if someone actually saw the risen Christ?

In Luke 16, Jesus told a parable to the Pharisees, "who loved money" (Luke 16:14). The parable spoke of a rich man who had died and went to Hades, the place of torment, and a poor man who had died and was comforted because he was at Abraham's side. The rich man first asked Abraham for some comfort. But Abraham told him that there was a great chasm fixed between him and Hades, and that the chasm could not be crossed.

The rich man then asked that his relatives be warned of this torment: "'Then I beg you, father, send Lazarus to my family, for I have five brothers. Let him warn them, so that they will not also come to this place of torment.' Abraham replied, 'They have Moses and the Prophets; let them listen to them.' 'No, father Abraham,' he said, 'but if someone from the dead goes to them, they will repent.' He said to him, 'If they do not listen to Moses and the Prophets, they will not be convinced even if someone rises from the dead'" (Luke 16:27–31).

No clearer statement could be made about the convincing impact of the visible or historical evidence for the resurrection. Jesus is telling the Pharisees that their problem is not that they need evidence concerning the resurrection. Such evidence would be for them utterly unconvincing. Instead, says Jesus, "If they do not listen to Moses and the Prophets, they will not be convinced even if someone rises from the dead."

Historical evidence for the resurrection should not be shunned.

It can take its proper place in discussions about the resurrection of Christ. But, as Christ himself reminds us, unless we hear "Moses and the Prophets"—that is, unless we hear and believe what God himself has said in his Word, there will be no way to convince someone of the resurrection of Christ, even if they could witness it themselves! This takes us back, as we should expect by now, to our first chapter. The reason we believe the resurrection of Christ is the same reason anyone else will believe it, because, by God's grace through faith in Christ, we hear the Word of God as he speaks to us in Scripture.

Jesus Christ is alive. He now reigns in his spiritual body in the heavenlies. The "life principle" that began at creation with the inbreathing of God can continue only because the one who should not have died, because he did not sin, died for us in order that we who are "dead in [our] transgressions and sins" (Eph. 2:1) would live in him.

Without the resurrection, there is no Christianity. Without the resurrection, there is no life. Christ, who alone is the life (John 14:6), is the only way to true eternal life with him. Because he lives, we who are in him also live—forever.

Questions for Reflection

1. How does Scripture make clear that the resurrection of Christ was a public event?
2. Why couldn't Jesus just come to earth and give life to any who trust him? Why did he have to be raised from the dead?
3. What do you think is the most significant objection to the resurrection of Christ? How would you respond to it?

Recommended Reading

Bavinck, Herman. *Reformed Dogmatics: Sin and Salvation in Christ*. Vol. 3. ed. John Bolt and John Vriend. Grand Rapids: Baker Academic, 2006, 431–51.

Carson, D. A. *Scandalous: The Cross and Resurrection of Jesus*. Wheaton, IL: Crossway, 2010.

Gaffin, Richard B., Jr. *The Centrality of the Resurrection: A Study in Paul's Soteriology*. Grand Rapids: Baker, 1978.

Machen, J. Gresham. "The Resurrection of Christ." In *Historic Christianity*, 66–78. Philadelphia: Skilton House Ministries—Sowers, 1979.

Pictet, Benedict. "Of the Resurrection and Ascension of Christ," in *Christian Theology*. trans. Frederick Reyrou. Philadelphia: Presbyterian Board of Publication, n.d., 262–71.

CHAPTER 6

WHY BELIEVE IN SALVATION?

The story of Louie Zamperini remained relatively obscure for decades until Laura Hillenbrand happened on a newspaper article about him. Hillenbrand made a habit of reading old newspaper articles in order to glean facts and information for her work.

As she was perusing a vintage newspaper, she noticed an article about a man named Louie Zamperini and his running prowess. She became fascinated with Zamperini, and she wondered what had happened to him since his running days. The more she explored Zamperini's life, the more amazing his story became.

She eventually had the opportunity to meet Zamperini, and she was convinced that his story needed to be told. Her book on Zamperini's life, *Unbroken*, debuted at No. 2 on the New York Times bestseller list and remained on the list for almost four years.[1]

The book chronicles Zamperini's life, from his running days to his post-war life. Zamperini was on his way to an Olympic medal in running. Unfortunately for him, the Olympics, slated to be in Tokyo, had to be canceled because war had broken out with Japan. More unfortunately for him, Zamperini was drafted into the war and shot down at sea. He spent forty-seven days fighting for his life at sea aboard a life raft before being "rescued" by the Japanese. His stories of abuse and torture in Japanese prison camps are almost beyond belief. Equally beyond belief is the fact that he lived to tell it all.

But war took its toll on Zamperini. By the time he returned home, he was emotionally and physically spent. He was plagued by nightmares of his captors. The torture he was forced to endure did not end when he returned home, it merely changed location, from his body to his mind. His days and nights were filled with the mental torture of his memories, and he sought to dispel his demons through alcohol.

Louie's wife was deeply distressed over his post-war condition. She noticed at one point that Billy Graham was coming to town. She determined to find a way to coax Louie into going with her to hear Graham. Reluctantly, Louie went along. He listened as Graham began to preach from the gospel of John, chapter 8.

> Inside himself, Louie felt something twisting. "Darkness doesn't hide the eyes of God," Graham said. "God takes down your life from the time you were born to the time you die. And when you stand before God on the great judgment day, you're going to say, 'Lord I wasn't such a bad fellow,' and they are going to pull down the screen and they are going to shoot the moving picture of your life from the cradle to the grave, and you are going to hear every thought that was going through your mind every minute of the day, every second of the minute, and you're going to hear the words that you said. And your own words, and your own thoughts, and your own deeds, are going to condemn you as you stand before God on that day. And God is going to say, 'Depart from me.'"[2]

This was not good news to Louie. He knew, deep down, that if God began to number all of Louie's faults and sins, he would fail miserably; he would be unable to pass the test. "Louie felt indignant rage flaring in him, a struck match. *I am a good man*, he thought. *I am a good man.* Even as he had this thought, he felt the lie in it."[3] Louie had heard all he wanted to hear that night. He returned home to the nightmares and mental torture that had become so familiar to him.

Louie's wife, Cynthia, urged him to come with her again the next night. Louie refused. He had heard enough. But Cynthia persisted. Louie agreed to go on one condition. As soon as Graham would call his audience to bow their heads and pray, they would leave.

When Graham finished preaching that night, Louie grabbed Cynthia and they headed for the gate. Suddenly, another disturbing memory came to mind: "He was a body on a raft, dying of thirst. He felt words whisper from his swollen lips. It was a promise thrown at heaven, a promise he had not kept, a promise he had allowed himself to forget until just this instant: *If you will save me, I will serve you forever.* And then, standing under a circus tent on a clear night in downtown Los Angeles, Louie felt rain falling. It was the last flashback he would ever have. Louie let go of Cynthia and turned toward Graham. He felt supremely alive. He began walking. 'This is it,' said Graham. 'God has spoken to you. You come on.'"[4]

From that day until Louie's death in 2014, his life was never the same; he was a changed man. The nightmares were gone for good, the alcohol was no longer appealing, and Louie lived out the next five decades in service to the Lord who had changed him.

The story of Louie Zamperini is dramatic in almost every way. A superior athlete robbed of his chance for glory; a war hero robbed of his humanity; a war veteran robbed of his sanity. But then he was changed. He heard the good news of the gospel, he trusted in the Lord Jesus Christ, and everything that he once was paled into insignificance compared to what he had become. He was a new man.

Louie Zamperini's story is not typical. If it were typical, it would not be the stuff of bestselling books and blockbuster movies. But it is not the atypical aspects of Louie's life that are most important. The most important aspect of Louie's entire life was that God saved him. It is this salvation that will be our focus in this chapter. What we will see is that, even for lives that are "typical," the same kind of change that Louie experienced is needed for each and every one of us.

Reasons

The God Who Saves

Before we look at the central aspects of salvation, we have to discuss briefly just who this God is who saves people from their sins.

After Jesus rose from the dead and before he went back to his Father, he gave his disciples this instruction: "Then Jesus came to them and said, 'All authority in heaven and on earth has been given to me. Therefore go and make disciples of all nations, baptizing them in the name of the Father and of the Son and of the Holy Spirit, and teaching them to obey everything I have commanded you. And surely I am with you always, to the very end of the age'" (Matt. 28:18–20).

Christians through the centuries have acknowledged that the God who saves, and the God that is worshiped, is one God who is three distinct persons. Jesus tells his disciples that any who would follow him must be baptized into the (one) name of Father, Son, and Holy Spirit.

Unlike any other religion in the world, Christianity recognizes that the New Testament requires Christians to have the name of God, which is Father, Son, and Holy Spirit, placed upon them through baptism. This means that we identify with that name. It also means that when Christians speak of God, they mean One who is Father, Son, and Holy Spirit.

This is a deep mystery, unfathomable by the human mind. Just exactly how one God can be three persons, each of whom is fully God, is beyond our ability to grasp. Without this truth, however, no salvation is possible.

Because God is three in one, there are different activities undertaken by each one. Jesus wanted his disciples to understand this mysterious truth before he was taken to the cross. So, as he gathered his disciples in an upper room, he began to talk to them about the Trinity. Those discussions, recorded for us in John 13–17, tell us much about each of the three persons and their distinct saving activities.

If we were to summarize those activities, we could say that the Father is the one who sends the Son; the Son is the one who comes, as a man, to suffer, die, rise, and ascend; and the Spirit comes to glorify the Son and to apply the salvation that the Son accomplished.

This is the glory of the Trinity. Without God as triune, there is no possibility of salvation. If God is to accomplish salvation, all three persons must be active. All three must be determined to save us.

Much more could be said about the Triunity of God, but enough is said here to allow us to see the Son of God, the second person of the Trinity, as the focus of the accomplishment of salvation for his people.

The "People" Problem

When Christians speak of "salvation," we can see immediately that something is wrong. The word "salvation" always indicates some kind of deliverance or rescue. People are saved from disasters and dire predicaments. People who have no problems or experience no dangers are not in need of salvation from anything.

The first thing that has to be understood about the Christian notion of salvation is that it points to a universal human condition. That condition is typically spoken of as "sin."

One of the reasons we needed to begin this book with chapters that deal with the Bible and with God is that we cannot understand what salvation is until we see what the Bible tells us about who God is, who we are, and what God has done.

Human beings are not the product of a random process of accidental mutations. We did not become "people" because time and matter randomly formed us. If that were the case, as we will see in future chapters, then nothing of any meaning can be affirmed by or about human beings. If we accidentally bubbled up from nonhuman matter, then we are no more "meaningful" than the random fizz of a can of soda.

The Bible's account of the origin of human beings is full of meaning and purpose for us. It opens with the account of creation. For five days, God creates the world and the living creatures he chose to inhabit his world. The climax of that creation is the creation of human beings. When God creates for the first five days, he simply speaks and creates. But the sixth day is different. On the sixth day, God takes counsel with himself. He says, "Let us make mankind in our image" (Gen. 1:26).[5]

We soon discover that to be "image of God" means (at least)

that the man and the woman will have responsibilities given to them by God. The other living creatures that God made were given a command to be fruitful and multiply, but they have no moral responsibility to obey. What God commands them to do, they will do.

Adam and Eve are also commanded to be fruitful and multiply. Unlike the rest of the living creatures, however, they are commanded to subdue the earth, to have dominion over it. They are to rule, in other words, as "little lords" under the sovereign lordship of the God who made them. This command was given only to human beings.

Adam and Eve were also given a negative command. They were to rule over the creatures God had created and to subdue the earth. But there was one thing—one tree—that they were not to touch. In other words, God defined their rule over the earth in a way that recognized that God himself was the true sovereign. He picked out one tree which they could not rule over or subdue, and from which they were not to eat (Gen. 2:16–17).

If Adam and Eve had obeyed God's commands, they would have, eventually, been able to partake of eternal life (Gen. 3:24). But Eve, and Adam with her (Gen. 3:6), was tempted by Satan. They both succumbed to the temptation to eat from the tree that God had picked out as forbidden. They had deceived themselves (2 Cor. 11:3) into thinking that they really were in control of the entire Garden. God had given them dominion over everything except that one tree. Satan convinced them that God was wrong and that the tree would be helpful to them. So they ate.

When Adam and Eve ate from the forbidden tree, everything in the "very good" Garden in which God had placed them began to fall apart. For the first time, Adam and Eve were ashamed, and they covered themselves. They could no longer live in the Garden completely open to each other. They had to hide themselves from each other.

Even worse, when God came down to the Garden after they had sinned, they heard him, and they tried to hide from God. They thought they could go to a place where God could not find them.

What happened after Adam and Eve violated God's command comprises the rest of the history of mankind. Because their sin was an attempt to usurp God's authority, God had to punish them. The serpent, as the vehicle of Satanic temptation, was punished. Eve was punished with the pain of childbirth and with conflict in her relationship with Adam (Gen. 3:16). Adam was punished with the promise of difficult and painful work. The earth, which was his and Eve's to rule prior to their sin, was now going to fight against them. When Adam fell, so did the rest of creation (cf. Rom. 8:19–22).

From that time forward, beginning with Cain and Abel, all people are born sinful. Because Adam was designated as the representative of all human beings, his sin is credited to all of humanity after him. The violent sin of Cain toward his own brother is just the beginning of a fallen human race that will find itself in perpetual opposition to its Creator. Any perusal of humanity at any point in history proves the universality of sin.

God gave life as a gift to Adam. He breathed life into him (Gen. 2:7) and then created Eve from his very substance. They were both created to live.

But their disobedience, as God had promised them (Gen. 2:17), brought sure and certain death. The penalty for rebellion against the Gracious Lifegiver was that life itself would be taken away. Existence would continue, but the true life that God gave to Adam and Eve so that they might have perfect fellowship with him evaporated on the day they ate of the forbidden tree.

Toil and pain and curse and chaos became the "normal" way of life, once sin shattered the goodness of God's Garden. Since their treacherous rebellion, no one is good; no one is righteous. Everyone is under the curse that Adam brought to humanity (see Rom. 3:9–18).

When Louis Zamperini wanted to suppress the words of Billy Graham's sermon, he tried to convince himself by repeating, "*I am a good man. I am a good man.*" But he knew, deep inside, that he wasn't a good man at all. No person is good in the eyes of God. We may try to convince ourselves that we're good compared to someone else. In reality, it is not "someone else" that we have sinned against. Our sin is against God, and him alone (Ps. 51:4). When we compare ourselves to him, we fail constantly, utterly, and miserably.

Adam's and Eve's failure was due to just one sinful act. But one sinful act is still sin, and it is treasonous. It defies the One who made us and whose character we are supposed to "image." As the Bible reminds us, "Whoever keeps the whole law and yet stumbles at just one point is guilty of breaking all of it" (James 2:10). Sin is a violation of God's character. Once his character is violated, we stand as guilty rebels before him.

Zamperini knew he had rebelled against God. Deep down, we all know the same thing (Rom. 1:32). We know that we cannot measure up to God's perfect standard. Like Zamperini, many still convince themselves that they are basically good people. Sure, there have been "mistakes." But there is always someone more "mistaken" than we are. Besides, we say to ourselves, look at the "good" things we have done!

Sin is universal. All of us are plagued with it. Instead of trying to hold down that truth by pretending we're somehow "good enough" for God, the beginning of the good news of salvation is that we recognize and acknowledge the bad news of our sin and depravity. We have to recognize that, in spite of what we might want to think about ourselves, we really are not good people at all. We are, in fact, slaves to our own sin (Rom. 6:16). We rebel against God and his character every day. Instead of doing all things to his glory, we seek our own glory. We need to be freed. We need salvation.

The first reason we should believe in salvation is that all of us need it. Salvation is not meant for the really wicked, or for those we think are worse than we are. As with Adam and Eve, one sin brings death as its proper penalty. Unlike Adam and Eve, we not only commit sin, but sin has spread from them to us. As the Bible puts it, "One trespass resulted in condemnation for all people" (Rom. 5:18). From God's perspective, which is the true perspective, we are rebels against him. We need to be saved from ourselves.

The Divine Design

Once we acknowledge that sin is universal, that it continues in every person from the point of conception on (Ps. 51:5)—and that it is individual, that it plagues and enslaves me—we begin to see what Christians mean by "salvation."

Since sin is rebellion against a holy God, it is impossible that such a good and holy God could overlook that rebellion. Since he is holy, he must punish all violations of his character.

This concept of God goes against more "popular" notions of him. Typically, people think that God's love trumps everything else. He is not bothered by our rebellion. Others think God's primary job is to forgive us, no matter our attitude toward him.

We have to recognize who God is, not what we might want him to be. We must know him according to what he *says* he is and does. God says that "the one who sins is the one who will die" (Ezek. 18:20). He says that "the wages of sin is death" (Rom. 6:23), and the death that sin produces is not just physical death but eternal punishment (see Rev. 20:14, for example). The Lord is too holy to allow sin in his eternal presence. He cannot look upon, or tolerate, sin (Hab. 1:13).

An analogy here might help. Suppose you have a sworn enemy who had dedicated himself to opposing and fighting against all that you are and stand for. Anything that you hold dear he vehemently opposes. His disposition toward you includes a resolve to fight against everything you love. Now suppose this enemy claims that your responsibility is to accept him as he is, to bring him into your home, and to include him in all your affairs.

How would you respond to this person? At minimum, you would conclude that he is not thinking clearly. He cannot really think that he can oppose you at every turn and still expect that you will include him.

Now consider that God—who alone deserves praise and who is to be honored by all of his human creatures—simply decides to bring all who are opposed to him into his presence, where they can oppose him more vigorously. Their presence itself is a violation of his character, because it is sin and rebellion in the presence of perfect goodness and holiness. Is God expected to tolerate that rebellion? Is he supposed to bend to our desires?

When Moses and Isaiah (just to use two examples) find themselves in the presence of God, they are afraid and undone (see Ex. 3:6; Isa. 6:5). They recognize that they are not worthy to be in God's presence because they stand condemned in his sight. The very presence of God requires us, not God, to act differently.

But our sinful and rebellious condition does not have to be the end of our story. Even though we are the ones who defiled God's good creation, he graciously provided a way back to him. God gives a hint of this "way back to him" as soon as sin enters the world. He says to the serpent, "And I will put enmity between you and the woman, and between your offspring and hers; he will crush your head, and you will strike his heel" (Gen. 3:15). God declares that there will be animosity and antagonism between the seed of the serpent (Satan) and the seed of the woman. The seed of the serpent (Satan) will strike the heel of the seed of the woman. In other words, someone who is a descendant of the woman will be wounded. The good news is that this descendant will crush the head of the seed of the serpent. In other words, the seed of the woman will destroy the seed of the serpent.

After God pronounced his curses on the serpent, the woman, and the man, he "made garments of skin for Adam and his wife and clothed them" (Gen. 3:21). This may seem like a mere gesture of kindness. But it is much more than that. Adam and Eve had already made coverings for themselves by sewing fig leaves together (Gen. 3:7). The process of sewing these leaves together indicates that they had adequately accomplished their purpose. They were no longer exposed.

Why, then, did God make garments of skin for Adam and Eve, since they were already covered? Those garments provided a hint as to what God would do to solve the sin problem that Adam brought into the world. There are two aspects to the covering that God made that help us see his grand design for salvation, in light of sin.

1. First, the problem of sin could not be "covered" by the efforts of Adam and Eve. If they were going to be truly covered, God would have to cover them.

2. The covering that God provided, unlike the covering that Adam and Eve made, required a sacrifice that God himself would initiate.

The covering that Adam and Eve needed was a covering, not one they made, but that God made. God made a covering of animal skin, not leaves. It required an animal sacrifice to properly cover them. This points to the fact that if sin is going to be covered, blood will have to be shed (Heb. 9:22). In other words, the death that sin brings can be covered only by the death that bloodshed requires.

These two key aspects of God's activity toward Adam and Eve are developed in God's dealings with humanity from this point forward. We see, in Genesis 4, that Abel brings an acceptable sacrifice to the Lord; it is a sacrifice that required the shedding of blood. But Cain's sacrifice consists of the "fruits of the soil" (Gen. 4:3); it is not acceptable to God. Already we begin to see that it is not simply *any* sacrifice to God that will do. The only sacrifice that can truly cover our sin is a sacrifice that God initiates, that he can accept, and includes the shedding of blood.

The rest of the Bible illustrates these two key aspects of salvation—that God will provide an acceptable sacrifice, and that sin cannot be covered without the death which the shedding of blood requires.

Certain events in biblical history demonstrate this more clearly. In Genesis 22, for example, God calls Abraham to sacrifice his only son, Isaac (Gen. 22:1–18). So Abraham takes Isaac to Mount Moriah to sacrifice him to the Lord. As far as Abraham knows, God requires the shedding of a blood sacrifice to cover his sin.

We know from this chapter, though Abraham does not yet

know, that God is doing this to test Abraham. He wants Abraham to demonstrate his loyalty to him. Abraham knew that God had promised to build and bless a nation through Isaac, so he realized that God could raise Isaac from the dead (Heb. 11:17–19). Abraham proves himself to be obedient to the Lord. Once Abraham's obedience is proven, God stops Abraham from going through with the sacrifice of his son. Instead, God provides an animal, a ram, for Abraham to sacrifice. Abraham names that place "The LORD Will Provide" (Gen. 22:14).

With this event, we begin to see in more detail the two aspects of God's plan of salvation. Not only must *God* provide an acceptable sacrifice, and not only must there be the shedding of blood (i.e., death) for sin to be properly covered, but we see hints, from the perspective of the New Testament, that this shedding of blood must be more than the shedding of the blood of animals. For human sin to be covered, there must be the shedding of human blood—someone must die—and it must all be acceptable to and provided by God himself.

Divine Determination

We can now see that human beings, who were created as image of God, rebel against the God who made them and in whose image they are supposed to be. That rebellion mars and distorts the image of God. It takes away from the glory of God as it was meant to be "reflected" in people who are his image. So God must punish sin. If God did not punish sin, he would not be holy. And if God were not holy, he would not be God.

The good news is that God's attitude toward sin is not only to punish it. God also determines to cover the sin that we have brought into the world. That covering requires the shedding of blood; it requires death. More specifically, it requires the shedding of blood by way of a sacrifice that is acceptable to God.

How can a sinful person offer a perfectly acceptable sacrifice to God? The answer is, no mere human being can offer such a sacrifice. Why, then, did God require his people in the Old Testament to offer sacrifices? The author of the book of Hebrews gives us an answer to that question.

> The high priest entered the inner room, and that only once a year, and never without blood, which he offered for himself and for the sins the people had committed in ignorance. . . . This is an illustration for the present time, indicating that the gifts and sacrifices being offered were not able to clear the conscience of the worshiper. They are only a matter of food and drink and various ceremonial washings—external regulations applying until the time of the new order. (Heb. 9:7, 9–10)

The ritual of the high priest in the Old Testament was not meant to clear away the guilt of sin. That ritual was external, and it was meant to be temporary. It was pointing the Lord's people to the real sacrifice that was not temporary, but eternal.

> But when Christ came as high priest of the good things that are now already here, he went through the greater and more perfect tabernacle that is not made with human hands, that is to say, is not a part of this creation. He did not enter by means of the blood of goats and calves; but he entered the Most Holy Place once for all by his own blood, thus obtaining eternal redemption. (Heb. 9:11–12)

Christ entered the perfect tabernacle—that is, the holy presence of God. He could not enter God's presence through the blood of goats and calves. Animal blood was not sufficient for entering the glory of God's presence. As the God-man, he could enter only by his own blood.

> For Christ did not enter a sanctuary made with human hands that was only a copy of the true one; he entered heaven itself, now to appear for us in God's presence. Nor did he enter heaven to offer himself again and again, the way the high priest enters the Most Holy Place every year with blood that is not his own. Otherwise Christ would have had to suffer many times since the creation of the world. But he has appeared once for all at the culmination of the ages to do away with sin by the sacrifice of himself. (Heb. 9:24–26)

What Hebrews is telling us brings us to the glorious conclusion of what we saw in the Old Testament. God sacrificed animals to cover Adam and Eve. Abraham was told to sacrifice his own son. He was stopped just before that sacrifice and was reminded that God would provide the sacrifice needed to cover sins. That sacrifice, we now see, is God-in-the-flesh, Jesus Christ, the son of God.

This is why the celebrations of Christmas and of Easter are so important. They should really be seen as one celebration, not two. The coming of Christ without the resurrection does not conquer sin. Resurrection without the perfect sacrifice of God's own incarnate Son is not acceptable. There has to be the shedding of blood.

Christmas is not meant to be about reindeer and a jolly old elf. Christmas, as the word indicates, is about Christ. The coming of Christ was the fulfillment of all of history, since that fateful day when our first parents decided to rebel against their Creator and eat the fruit he had forbidden. The focus of Christmas has to begin here:

But after he had considered this, an angel of the Lord appeared to him in a dream and said, "Joseph son of David, do not be afraid to take Mary home as your wife, because what is conceived in her is from the Holy Spirit. She will give birth to a son, and you are to give him the name Jesus, because he will save his people from their sins." All this took place to fulfill what the Lord had said through the prophet: "The virgin will conceive and give birth to a son, and they will call him Immanuel" (which means "God with us"). (Matt. 1:20–23)

Christmas celebrates God with us. The way that God provided his presence with us was that God the Son would become one of us. He would, while he remained God, become man.

The Son of God became man to identify with us. In that way, he was like Adam. As man, he learned what it means to obey God (Heb. 5:8). Unlike Adam, he obeyed perfectly. He came to do what Adam failed to do. This is one reason why Scripture calls him "the last Adam" (1 Cor. 15:45).

Not only did the last Adam, the Son of God, obey throughout his life; his obedience could not end there. Because Adam brought death to a world that was full of life, the last Adam had to overcome the death penalty that sin required. He had to overcome the death that rebellion deserves. So, says Scripture about Christ, "Being found in appearance as a man, he humbled himself by becoming obedient to death—even death on a cross!" (Phil. 2:8). He lived a perfect life; he died a perfectly obedient death. In doing so, he brought life—he was the life (John 14:6)—to a world full of death.

The sacrifice that God requires was now met in the Son. It was met because God provided it. He provided it in his own Son. And it was met because the sacrifice that God provided was a perfect sacrifice. A perfect sacrifice is something no human being could offer. But Christ was not only a human being; he was the God-man, God with us. He alone was able to accomplish what we could not accomplish in order to provide a solution to the problem that we ourselves perpetuate in the world.

Response

The question that should come to mind at this point is, "So what?" We've seen who God is, who we are as rebellious sinners, and what God has done about our sin. Are these just interesting facts for us to ponder, or perhaps to approve?

The fact is, unless we respond properly to what God has done, we will remain in our sins and will suffer the deserved penalty, which is eternal death (Rom. 6:23). The fact of who God is and of what Christ has done has to be applied to us to be effective in and for us.

The apostle Paul and his traveling partner Silas found themselves imprisoned because of their preaching of the gospel. One night an earthquake hit, and it opened the prison doors. The man who was in charge of guarding the prisoners was about to kill himself because he feared that his prisoners had escaped, which would require his superiors to put him to death. Paul called to him to stop, because the prisoners were all still behind bars.

At this, the jail guard asked Paul and Silas, "Sirs, what must I do to be saved?" They replied, 'Believe in the Lord Jesus, and you will be saved—you and your household'" (Acts 16:25–31).

In order for the salvation that God has provided to be applied, we must believe in the Lord Jesus Christ. To believe in Christ does not simply mean to believe all of the things we have discussed in this chapter. It does mean that, but it means much more than that.

It means that we are to trust Christ, to recognize and acknowledge that we are rebels, that we have sinned against God and his character. It means to acknowledge, like Louie Zamperini, that we are not good, we are wicked and obstinate toward the God who made us and who provided salvation.

When we trust Christ, we place ourselves—our very lives each and every day—into his hands. We say to him, "I renounce my own sin. I repent of my rebellion against you. I resolve to follow you, and I know that you alone have saved me from my sins." When we say that, we open our Bibles, and we begin to follow him according to what he has said. We find a church that preaches this very gospel so that we might grow in our faith with other believers. This is the lifestyle of those who have salvation, who have been saved from their sin.

When we respond in this way, it means we have been changed by God himself. He transports us from the darkness of our sin to the light of his glorious grace. Like the blind whom Jesus healed, we begin to see things properly for the first time. We see the world as God's world, ourselves as his willing and dependent creatures, and we see Christ, our Savior, as the only one capable of delivering us from eternal peril.

Conclusion

We believe in salvation because without it, we perish. We don't believe in salvation because someone has concocted a way to pretend we are acceptable to God. As a matter of fact, no other religion in all the world even comes close to recognizing the truths we have discussed in this chapter. Every other religion is tailored to the ability of human beings to get themselves to the "right" place, either by earning it by a "good" life, or by focusing on the proper things, or by "letting go" to let God. None of these approaches can cover our rebellious sin against a holy God.

The salvation offered in Christianity is not at all like other religions. "As it is written: 'What no eye has seen, what no ear has heard, and what no human mind has conceived'—the things God has prepared for those who love him—these are the things God has revealed to us by his Spirit" (1 Cor. 2:9–10). No eye has seen, nor ear heard the salvation that comes only through Christ. That salvation is understood only because God has revealed it to us in his Word and by his Spirit.

Louis Zamperini had multiple reasons to live his life as a tortured and bitter victim. His quest for Olympic gold was halted. He was forsaken at sea, beaten and tortured by the enemy, and experienced things that few human beings could survive. According to Laura Hillenbrand, however, after he was converted, Louie "remained infectiously, incorrigibly cheerful. He once told a friend that the last time he could remember being angry was some forty years before."[6] When God reaches into and changes a human heart, life radically changes. That's what salvation does, and that's why all of us desperately need it. We believe in the salvation that God offers and has provided, because without it, there is no hope.

Apart from this salvation, nothing but punishment and pain await us. With Christ as our Savior, we can look forward to final and complete removal of all pain and sorrow. As the apostle John says, "Then I saw 'a new heaven and a new earth,' for the first heaven and the first earth had passed away, and there was no longer any sea. I saw the Holy City, the new Jerusalem, coming down out of heaven from God, prepared as a bride beautifully dressed for her husband. And I heard a loud voice from the throne saying, 'Look!

God's dwelling place is now among the people, and he will dwell with them. They will be his people, and God himself will be with them and be their God. "He will wipe every tear from their eyes. There will be no more death" or mourning or crying or pain, for the old order of things has passed away'" (Rev. 21:1–4).

Salvation offers true hope for today and true rest for eternity. To shun such a gracious offering, which only God can provide, is the height of human foolishness.

Questions for Reflection

1. What would God be like if he did not punish sin?
2. Why is death *deserved* for those who sin?
3. What is the difference between just *believing* in Christ and *trusting* him?
4. What are some reasons why someone would not want to trust Christ and be saved from their sins?

Recommended Reading

Piper, John. *Finally Alive.* Fearn, UK: Christian Focus, 2009.

Sproul, R. C. *What Is Faith? Crucial Questions.* Sanford, FL: Reformation Trust, 2010.

Sproul, R. C. *Can I Be Sure I'm Saved? Crucial Questions.* Sanford, FL: Reformation Trust, 2010.

Oliphint, K. Scott, and Sinclair B. Ferguson. *If I Should Die Before I Wake: What's Beyond This Life?* Fearn, UK: Christian Focus, 2005.

CHAPTER 7

WHY BELIEVE IN LIFE AFTER DEATH?

If you look at almost any poll about life after death, it will show that the vast majority of people believe in an afterlife. A recent CBS news poll asked more than a thousand adults in America about belief in the afterlife. Three out of four Americans believe in the existence of heaven or hell. When asked where they thought they would spend the afterlife, 82 percent of those polled believed they would spend it in heaven.[1]

Given these statistics, it might seem like a chapter on the afterlife is not needed. After all, if 75 percent of Americans believe in an afterlife and 82 percent of Americans believe they will spend eternity in heaven, why bother asking why?

The reason that it's worth the bother is that these polls never get around to asking the "why" question. This is a significant omission. If three out of four of us believe in an afterlife, wouldn't it be helpful and useful to know why most of us believe this? As difficult as it is to get 75 percent of a population to agree on anything, an agreement like this one should certainly be investigated.

In light of this overwhelming consensus, books on people who claim to have experiences of heaven do very well. *Heaven Is for*

Real: A Little Boy's Astounding Story of His Trip to Heaven and Back by Todd Burpo and Lynn Vincent hit No. 1 on the "USA Today's Best-Selling Books" list and was later made into a movie. Books such as *Proof of Heaven: A Neurosurgeon's Journey into the Afterlife* by Eben Alexander, *To Heaven and Back: A Doctor's Extraordinary Account of Her Death, Heaven, Angels, and Life Again: A True Story* by Mary Neal, and *90 Minutes in Heaven: A True Story of Death and Life* by Don Piper have all sold remarkably well. So far, only one, *The Boy Who Came Back From Heaven* by Alex Malarkey, was admitted by its author to be "malarkey" and thus was retracted.

What makes these books so popular? Is it the fact that so many already believe in an afterlife? Or could it be that so many who believe in an afterlife are looking for reasons for their belief? My own suspicion is that many who affirm some kind of existence after death are looking for evidence for that belief. Jeffrey Long, a medical doctor, set out to find empirical evidence for life after death, and he claims to have found it. His book *Evidence of the Afterlife* spent time on the New York Times bestseller list in 2010.

Even in light of this overwhelming consensus, there have always been some who prefer to argue that death is the end of everything. When the late Christopher Hitchens, the brilliant writer and atheist, discovered he had terminal cancer, his assessment of death was simply, "Hello darkness my old friend."[2] True to his chosen beliefs, Hitchens was convinced that the only thing remaining after death was darkness. But how many funerals feature "The Sound of Silence" in their liturgy? Hitchens represents only 25 percent of the population. For the rest, we believe that there is light, not darkness, at the end of the life tunnel.

Reasons

The question of "why" is virtually absent from discussions of our popular belief in the afterlife. We all recognize that there really is no current evidence for life after death. Even Jeffrey Long, in his book, had to admit that the empirical "evidence" that he was able to collect was not evidence of life after death, but of experiences by many people who were "near death." For him, so many "near death" experiences were enough to convince him that there had to be life after death. But that seems to be a significant leap. An experience from people who are near death, even if there are thousands of them that are exactly alike, tells us nothing about what happens after we all die. It only tells us what "near death" patients experience. In light of no evidence, why do people continue to believe in life after death?

As a matter of fact, there is an incredibly strong and influential tradition in the West for believing in the afterlife. There have been two traditions that have instilled in Western culture the notion of life after death. The first tradition is Christianity. We will discuss that a little later.

But much of the general belief about the afterlife can be traced all the way back to Greek philosophy. Greek philosophy did have one tradition that argued for no afterlife at all. Once the body died, some taught, it was dead and nothing remained of that person.[3] But there was another stronger tradition that argued that we should all believe in an immortal soul. That view has been predominant for millennia.

Even if the name Plato is unfamiliar to us, much of what he, and the Greek philosophical tradition, taught has been embraced and has filtered down to the rest of us over hundreds of years. It was Greek philosophy that made famous and familiar the notion of a "soul."

Problems with Persons

Greek philosophy took for granted that there was some kind of "animating," or life-giving, aspect to human beings. Plato thought that this aspect—the soul—was immortal. He thought that souls preexisted their bodies, then inhabited a body in history, then existed after the body had died. The notion of the soul's preexistence is rarely discussed. But the idea that there is a soul, and that it continues after we die, is still the majority opinion in the West.

Even if we have never read or heard of Greek philosophy, even if we have no time for philosophical discussion, most of us recognize that there is something in each person that is significantly distinct from physical appearance. Philosophers have spilled gallons of ink trying to find out exactly what it is that continues if our lives continue after death. Some philosophers, of course, because of their commitment to naturalism (i.e., nature is all there is), think that nothing continues after death. David Hume, the empirical naturalist we mentioned in chapter 4, was forced to conclude that human beings were just a "bundle of ideas" that died when the body died.

Because of the influence of Plato and others, however, many philosophers have believed that human beings are a duality of body and soul (or body and mind). This view, though, has been terribly hard to prove for a couple of reasons. The first reason is that philosophy, by and large, begins its task by assuming that it can, by itself, adequately define what a person is. But this has proven to be notoriously difficult.

Some have wanted to make a distinction between a "human

being," which is purely biological, and a "person," which is identified in terms of "consciousness." In this distinction, there is a duality that composes us—our biological side, which makes us "human beings," and our psychological side, which makes us "persons." But philosophy has no way to account for something like "consciousness." It has never been able to establish that there are persons whose existence includes something beyond their physical traits.

Even with no proof or successful argument, the majority of people still agree that there is life after death. So there must be something obvious in the belief that our existence is, somehow, more than our bodies. But exactly what is that "more than"?

Have you ever asked yourself how you know that, for example, your sibling or your best friend is, right now, the same person he or she was ten years ago? Or five years ago? Or one year ago? What is it that makes us the same person even while our physical bodies grow and change, sometimes drastically?

Some have argued that it is memory that makes us the same person. But what happens if we lose our memories, or if we don't remember "enough" to make us the same person? How much memory is enough to make us the same person? Do the ravages of Alzheimer's disease mean we become, literally, someone else?

Others have said that what makes us the same person over time is "continuity of consciousness." But what could that mean, for example, when we lose a certain consciousness when we sleep or if we are subjected to a coma? Does that mean you become a different person once your consciousness is not continuous? How continuous does your consciousness have to be for you to be the same person?

For most of us, these questions are not troubling. Even if we can't find the answers to them, we just know that we are the same person we were a decade ago, that our siblings are the same people throughout their lives, that our long-time friends have not become different, or other, persons over time. Whether philosophers can provide an account of personhood or not, we know that there is continuity of persons through time.

The point we should recognize here is that we have a wildly popular belief in the reality of life after death even if there has yet to be given an adequate or successful reason for that belief. We know that we are persons, that we are more than just our physical selves. There is something that is different from the material that is our physical makeup.

One of the substantial influences for our belief in the afterlife is Christianity. Since, unlike philosophy and science, Christianity does have reasons for belief in the afterlife, this is another topic that shows how Christianity alone provides the rationale for what we believe. How do we justify a Christian belief in the afterlife?

Problems with Proofs

One of the most influential Christian arguments for the afterlife, historically, came from the pen of Bishop Joseph Butler (1692–1752). Butler wrote a highly influential book titled *The Analogy of Religion*. The purpose of the book was to try to convince the deists[4] of Butler's day that religion was not only natural, as the deists thought, but was supernatural as well. Butler wanted his deistic friends to affirm some kind of life beyond the natural.

In many ways, Butler's argument is similar to the arguments of philosophy. In the first chapter of his *Analogy*, which is titled "Of a Future Life," Butler argues that we all recognize that we use our reasoning and perceptive faculties (what he calls our "living powers") in this life, yet we do not know on what those "powers" depend. What Butler is saying is that we all use reason and perception, even over various changes in time, even though we don't know where they come from or how they are put into practice by us. Why should we think that death will destroy them? He says:

> As we are greatly in the dark, upon what the exercise of our living powers depends, so we are wholly ignorant what the powers themselves depend upon; the powers themselves as distinguished, not only from their actual exercise, but also from the present capacity of exercising them; and as opposed to their destruction. . . . Since then we know not at all upon what the existence of our living powers depends, this shows further, there can no probability be collected from the reason of the thing, that death will be their destruction: because their existence may depend upon somewhat in no degree affected by death.[5]

In other words, since we use our reason and our senses even though we have no idea of their source, can't we also recognize that there is a high probability that they will continue after our physical existence ceases?

Butler clearly states that "probability is the very guide of life."[6] We use our reason now. Thus, we should expect to use our reason after death.

Unfortunately, though Butler was attempting to provide Christian reasons for believing in a future life, he was never able to move beyond the weak and groundless arguments that philosophy had been presenting for hundreds of years. What Butler wanted to do was to say that since we recognize some things that seem to be the same in our lives, over time—things like our thinking and perceiving—it is probable that those things will continue after death.

But this is an argument with no teeth. It has its foundation in what we do not know, and it tries to move from what we don't know to some kind of probability that the things we don't know about will continue beyond death. Also, as we have seen in chapter 4, the notion of probability gets us nowhere. This is even more true when it is admitted, as Butler does, that we just don't know on what our reasoning and perceiving faculties depend. How can it be probable that they will continue after death when we have no idea how they function at all in this life?

There have to be better reasons for our belief in an afterlife than what the philosophers and Butler have to give us.

Christianity and Life

The reason that most people believe in life after death may be its prominence in Western philosophical discussions. Or it may be a side effect of a certain prominence of Christianity in Western history. Only the Christian position is able to give a full account of what it means to be a person and of what life as a person means. Since most people believe in an afterlife, it might be a good idea to begin with that belief when speaking with people who are skeptical of Christianity.

I remember reading, years ago, the "Humanist Manifesto II," which was written by the agnostics Paul Kurtz and Edwin Wilson. It was a manifesto that was meant to proclaim the beliefs of humanism. The manifesto declared that "Promises of immortal salvation or fear of eternal damnation are both illusory and harmful." Instead, it said, "Science affirms that the human species is an emergence from natural evolutionary forces." It also affirms that "there is no credible evidence that life survives the death of the body."

For the humanist, the notion of life after death is an illusion. Human beings emerged from natural forces. Once human life ends in death, there is nothing beyond. Both the origin and the destiny, the beginning and the end of a human being, point to nothing but darkness and the void. We started by a chance collection of "forces" in nature; there was no purpose for our existence, except that it just happened. Human beings are a cosmic collection of random events. Once this human accident is dead, since it came from nothing, absolutely nothing remains.

In reading through this Manifesto, however, this one line jumped off the page: "The preciousness and dignity of the individual person is a central humanist value."[7] Anyone who is alert to what this Manifesto is trying to say will be confused by this last affirmation. How is our life precious if it is merely accidental? The fact is that there can be no real dignity to a human being if it is only a chance-produced collection of temporal, dying materials. A person would have no more "preciousness and dignity" than a garbage heap. A garbage heap is a collection of material things that eventually decomposes and ceases to exist. How is a human being different from this, according to the humanist? How can you associate "preciousness and dignity" with a garbage heap?

The fact is, if you're going to be intellectually honest, you can't. Preciousness and dignity are terms that point beyond the material and the accidental. They require that there be something that is honorable and worthy of esteem. Material that eventually decomposes cannot produce dignity. There is only one way to ascribe dignity to human persons. They have to be more than their simple physical existence.

When we consider the reasons why Christians believe in a future life, we begin at the beginning. When we read about God's activity of creation in Genesis 1 and 2, we see that the climax of creation was the creation of man and woman in the image of God. For five days, God is simply saying, "Let there be . . . ," and there was. But on the last day, God takes counsel with himself. In doing so, he is marking the fact that what he is about to create is substantially different from what he has been creating. That difference, as we see in Genesis, is *not* in the material that God used to create Adam.

Like the animals, Adam was formed "from the dust of the ground." He was made from the same "stuff" as the animals. The difference for Adam (and, from him, Eve)—and it is a remarkable and profound difference—is that once God formed Adam from the dust of the ground, he "breathed into his nostrils the breath of life" (Gen. 2:7). We also learn that, because it was not good for Adam to be alone, God formed Eve from Adam, so that both of them were, in their creation, made as the image of God (see Gen. 1:27).

God created Adam in his image and, unlike the rest of creation, God breathed into Adam the breath of life. Humans bear the image of God and are given the breath of life—what nothing else in creation was given.

With Adam and Eve, their life was an inbreathed life. Unlike the animals, the life of Adam and Eve includes a special relationship to God, including certain responsibilities that God gave to them in the Garden. They were to tend the Garden under God. They were to be in charge of the day-to-day organization of the Garden, where God had placed them. They were to work, under God, as his servants and as lords over creation (Gen. 1:26). This is what "image of God" meant. And they were to keep themselves away from one particular tree that God designated to be off-limits.

If Adam and Eve had kept God's commandment to stay away from the forbidden tree, they would have continued forever to live in the Garden in perfect fellowship with God. There would have been no "life after death." There would have been no death. The inbreathed life that they had at the beginning would have continued without end. They would've been fruitful and multiplied as they tended the Garden—under God and in fellowship with him. They didn't obey God. They violated his commands and rebelled against the living relationship that he had established with them.

The rest of the Bible is a description of what God does because of Adam's sin. The first thing he does is curse them with death; the death that he had promised if they ate from the tree becomes a reality after sin. They are dust, and to dust they shall return (Gen. 3:19). But the death that Adam brought to creation is not the whole story. God provides a way for fellowship with him to continue. We learn early on that the Lord accepts the offering of Abel, but not of Cain. Even from the beginning, there was a way, an offering, that God would graciously accept so that a living fellowship with him could continue.

As the rest of Scripture unfolds, we begin to see that there are those who "walk with God" and who therefore are living in fellowship with God even at the end of their lives here on earth (see Gen. 5:24, for example). The clear teaching of Scripture is that the inbreathed life that God gave to Adam and Eve means that people will continue to exist beyond their earthly lives. That inbreathed, "image of God" life is an existence that will never end. Jesus makes clear to the Sadducees that when God calls himself the God of Abraham, Isaac, and Jacob, he is calling himself the God of those who are alive, not of the dead (Luke 20:37).

We also find out from Scripture that there is a stark division between those who die in Christ and are in fellowship with God, and those who don't. Jesus spoke of a man who died and was with Abraham, and another man who died but was in torment (Luke 16:19–31). In both cases, because each man was made in God's image, existence continues into eternity. For those who die in Christ, existence continues in him and with God. For those who die in their sins, existence continues, but it consists of nothing but eternal torment (see Luke 13:28–30).

It is clear from Scripture that "image of God" includes an inbreathed life, an inbreathed character, that is distinct from everything else in creation. It is distinct, centrally, in that it implies a relationship with God for eternity that ends either in eternal fellowship with him or in eternal torment under his wrath. The difference, as we have seen in a previous chapter, has to do with one's relationship to Christ. But in each and every case, human beings continue to exist beyond death. One either exists eternally with Christ, under God's grace, or one exists eternally in torment, under God's wrath. Once we begin to exist, the "life principle" that makes us "image of God" guarantees our eternal existence.

The CBS poll to which we referred in the beginning says that three-fourths of the population believe in heaven and hell. So, up to this point, much of what we have said is already affirmed by most adults. What is troubling about this poll is that 82 percent of these adults think they will spend eternity in heaven. This may betray a basic ignorance of the way of salvation, which we have already addressed. If all 82 percent were asked why they believe they will be in heaven, answers would vary significantly. Without the information that we have from Scripture, it is impossible to have a true and solid explanation for such a belief.

There are two more points that we need to recognize as we think about why we believe in life after death. These two points will not be as widely believed or known as belief in life after death. They do, however, give much more content to what Christians believe about life beyond the grave. The first point has to do with our original discussion about Greek philosophy and its idea of the immortality of the soul.

On occasion, when the topic comes up, I will ask a group this question: "What happens to the soul of a Christian when he dies?" The question is, in one sense, a trick question because it is designed to elicit a specific response. The typical answer that I get is, "It goes to heaven." Then I ask, "What is the 'it' that goes to heaven?" Sometimes the answer will be "the soul."

But this is not an accurate picture of the Christian view of life after death. The picture that Scripture gives us is not that when we die, some "thing" of ours goes to heaven. This is the problem with the Greek view of the soul and its immortality. It may be the case that there has been too much Greek influence on Christian thinking when it comes to these topics.

Instead, when we die, *we* go to be with Christ. In Paul's letter to the Philippians, he is telling the church, as he writes from prison, that it is possible that he will die. And he contrasts his life here with his life if he dies. He puts it this way, "I desire to depart and be with Christ, which is better by far; but it is more necessary for you that I remain in the body" (Phil. 1:23–24). The contrast here is between being in a far "better" place "with Christ," because of death, or remaining "in the body" on earth. Paul does not say that if he dies his soul will be with Christ. Rather, if he dies, he will be in a far better place with Christ, rather than remaining alive in the body on earth. Death brings us into a better place, but we should also see that death separates what was not initially meant to be rent asunder.

The biblical picture of our lives after death is not simply that "a soul" goes to heaven. Instead, we need to remember that our separation from our bodies when we die is an abnormal separation. It is a result of the entrance of sin in the world. If Adam and Eve had not sinned, there would have been no death, thus no separation of their existence from their bodily existence on earth.

For the Christian, to be "with Christ" after death is to be absent from the body. But there will be a time, at the end of time, when we will receive resurrected bodies. Because we have a "natural body," those who die in Christ will receive a "spiritual body" because Christ was raised from the dead (we will discuss this more in the next chapter). Thus, the time between our death and the end of time is commonly called the "intermediate state." What that means is that even though we live "with Christ" after our death, we have not yet become what we will be for eternity.

Typical pictures of life after death include things like people becoming angels, like Clarence in the movie *It's a Wonderful Life*. Pictures of people with wings playing harps on clouds are all too typical when it comes to depicting life after death. But the biblical picture is far different.

In Scripture, heaven is not our final destination. The place where Christians will reside for eternity is called "a new heaven and a new earth" (Rev. 21:1). That place will be a real place, an eternal place, where Christians, who have been in a "far better" place "with Christ," will finally be in the best possible place for eternity! At that time, which is the end of all time, "God's dwelling place is now among the people" (Rev. 21:3)—finally, fully, and completely.

The sad and terrible truth that must be recognized along with this glorious truth is that those who die in rebellion against God will experience, for eternity, the death that God promised to Adam and Eve. The death they will experience is called in Scripture the "second death" (Rev. 20:14; 21:8). Our physical death is not the end of our lives, but is the universal punishment for Adam's sin. But for those who die in Adam, and not in Christ, there is a second death awaiting. This second death is not an end, but an eternal existence. We continue to exist because, as image of God, God breathed that existence into all of us as Adam's children. The second death is the final and eternal punishment for sin. It is our existence in the "fiery lake of burning sulfur" (Rev. 21:8). It is the place that all of us deserve, since we all sin in Adam. It is the place that can be escaped only by trusting in Christ.

Existence after death is a fact of life. A majority of people believe it. The only real reason to believe it, however, is given to us in the Christian faith. Because God created people as his image, and thus breathed life into them, their existence will never cease. But existence after death is different from life after death. Life after death is found only in Christ. Without Christ, existence after death, though eternal, is called a "second death." Without these Christian truths, the best answer one has to the "why" question of life after death is "just because."

Responses

The primary objection to the idea of life after death is that there is no real evidence for it. Jeffrey Long tried to acquire evidence, but his evidence is only of near-death experiences, not death itself.

There is, however, evidence that there is life after death. As we have said in previous chapters, the Bible is a record of real historical events. These events did not take place in a hidden corner somewhere and go unrecorded. The Bible records numerous facts about life after death, including testimonies from some who actually saw those alive who had previously died (see Mark 9:2–8)! To say there is no evidence of life after death is to exclude the evidence the Bible gives, and has given, for thousands of years, almost since "the beginning." The objections that come against beliefs like this always have within them a bias against the very truth that would answer the objection. This should not hinder the Christian from responding to the objection. As a matter of fact, recognizing the presumed bias can help us understand how best to respond with biblical truth.

It is our status as "image of God" that alone can support our belief that there is more to us than our physical bodies, and that we, as persons, will exist for eternity. But because the "image of God" is defaced by the effects of sin, our existence can be restored to true life again only if we are, by faith, in Christ. Without that, our eternal existence will be nothing but torment. There is life after death. True life after death is found only in Christ, who himself died and now lives forever.

Questions for Reflection

1. What evidence is there that people are more than simply material bodies?
2. Why is it important for us to receive new spiritual bodies in the end?
3. Why do most people believe that they will spend life after death in heaven?

Recommended Reading

Hoekema, Anthony A. *The Bible and the Future*. Grand Rapids: Eerdmans, 1994.

Oliphint, K. Scott, and Sinclair B. Ferguson. *If I Should Die Before I Wake: What's Beyond This Life?* Fearn, UK: Christian Focus, 2005.

Piper, John. *Future Grace: The Purifying Power of the Promises of God*. Revised edition. Sisters, OR: Multnomah, 2012.

Sanders, John. *No Other Name: An Investigation into the Destiny of the Unevangelized*. Grand Rapids.: Eerdmans, 1992.

Sproul, R. C. *Unseen Realities: Heaven, Hell, Angels, and Demons*. Fearn, UK: Christian Focus, 2001.

CHAPTER 8

WHY BELIEVE IN GOD IN THE FACE OF MODERN SCIENCE?

I am routinely amazed at the lifestyle of twenty-first-century Westerners. I write on a small computer that I can move from room to room in a house that has multiple rooms with furniture, heat, and air-conditioning. When it is time for a break from typing, I go to the refrigerator to get food for lunch or to the coffee pot for a fresh cup. When the sun goes down, the lights go on. I can tune in to news that is "happening now" or watch a recent movie in my living room. If I get sick, I can call my doctor on the phone or drive to the hospital, where I will receive unprecedented care. When bedtime comes, I lay down on a comfortable mattress in a pest-free, climate-controlled house and have the opportunity to sleep all night.

If our response to these kinds of comforts is "So what," it may be that we lack perspective. One of the common plagues on modern Western society is its extreme shortsightedness. By that I mean that we have a strong, and perhaps even unconscious, tendency to see our present circumstances either as the best they have ever been or as the way things have always been. Generally speaking, when we consider our present circumstances, we lack a historical horizon to give us perspective.

From the vantage point of the history of humanity, however, most of what we do in our daily lives is brand-new. From the perspective of the history of the world, the vast majority of human beings would never have dreamed of the comforts and luxuries we use every day. For thousands and thousands of years, human beings had to spend the majority of their time working hard and long hours to obtain their own food, all the while enduring or succumbing to multiple illnesses and fighting against the harshness of the elements and their environment. The bulk of humanity had to focus on a single concern for survival each and every day. For thousands of years, when people prayed, "Give us this day our daily bread," they prayed it with earnest zeal and hope that there would be provision each day for their basic needs. Most of us no longer have to think in terms of "daily bread."

Perhaps we rarely, if ever, think of this comparison between now and the past. We tend to focus on the "now" of our own lives and our own lifetime. This kind of shortsightedness, what we might call historical myopia, is detrimental to us for at least two reasons.

First, whenever we ignore anything beyond our own circumstances, we tend to think that what is "now" is normal. The immediate becomes ultimate and absolute. There are numerous problems with this kind of thinking. We lose any kind of critical perspective on our own thinking and way of life. We lose the ability to see our lives, or our culture, or our "world," in the context of the circumstances and cultures of the past. Kids roll their eyes every time their parents say, "When I was young, I used to . . ."

Though it wearies the children, parents are teaching them that what is "now" has not always been the norm. Since we don't look past our own lifetime, what is normal is often confined to a seriously short period of time.

Second, when we lose historical perspective, we tend to think that what is new is always better. The amount of free time that Westerners currently enjoy is way beyond anything that would have been imagined for thousands of years. We no longer have to work long hours on our own land to produce our own food. We don't have to build our own homes or chop wood to ensure enough heat in them. From a historical perspective, most Westerners live luxurious lives. In one sense, today *is* better than the past.

But is our current situation better than the lifestyles of those who lived, say, in the eighteenth century? Some things are obviously better. The state of medicine is better; the ability to be more comfortable in our homes is better. Certainly, I would prefer to write this on a computer, which is much more forgiving of my mistakes, and thus more efficient, than to write on a typewriter or by hand!

Is newer always better? If we peer into humanity's past, we see that some of what we now enjoy has created newer and more serious problems. Constant access to the internet has contributed to the rise of global terrorism. How difficult would it be for those who hate the West to attack if there were no internet, no airplanes, no modern weapons, no media reports? Has the rise in "free time" created more opportunities for crime? Has the proliferation of pornography contributed to a cheapened and tawdry view of women and of children? Has it contributed to significant breakdowns in the family?

Now is not always normal. Newer is not always better.

Reasons

The title of this chapter is meant to give us a more historical perspective on the relationship of science to Christianity. As the title suggests, we are thinking about Christianity and our belief in it in light of modern science. Modern science, we could say, is, by definition, a recent phenomenon. Modern science began in the nineteenth century when science was defined and carried out in a radically different way than before. The word "scientist" was not even coined until the nineteenth century.

It is this focus that will give us two solid reasons why we believe in Christianity in light of modern science—the historical reason and the foundational reason. These two reasons are inextricably linked. They show that "now" is not always normal and that newer is not always better. First, the historical.

Historical

In its historical context, the relationship of science and Christian belief has been mostly harmonious, not hostile. Up until the modern period, the term "science" was not even used in the way that we now use it. Instead, the activity of discovering the workings of the world and its benefits was termed "natural philosophy" (or, sometimes, "natural theology").

It has been said that the Greek philosopher Thales (pronounced "Thay-lees"—c. 624–c. 546 BC) began the work of "science" when he accurately predicted a solar eclipse. In that prediction, Thales was observing the movements of the heavens and planets and was able to calculate when the moon would cover the light of the sun. This, by any definition, was what we now call "science," but it was done under the name of "natural philosophy."

Natural philosophy concerned itself with the workings of nature. It was a discipline that sought to discover and utilize the forces and laws of nature in order (1) to better understand how the world works and (2) to improve the quality of life for people. For most of Western history, science was a philosophical and/or theological endeavor, and its goal was to help aid our understanding of this world.

Any honest look at the work of "natural philosophy" for over two thousand years in the West will recognize that its goal was to connect the workings of the world with the "One" thing, or being, that could explain and justify those workings. In other words, "natural philosophy" intuitively recognized that there had to be something that provided for the harmonious display of nature, something that connected all of the different parts. In Greek philosophy, this "One" took on numerous and various identities.

Within a Christian context, however, when "natural philosophy" was pursued, it was recognized that "nature" was actually a "book," written by the one God, and that it was to be properly understood in light of what God said in *the* Book, the Bible. Nature was God's book and could be properly understood only when it was understood in light of his written book, the Bible.

The literature on this history is too vast to summarize, but we can see hints of it in three important examples. Francis Bacon (1561–1626) is credited with the application of the "scientific method," which highlighted the use of an inductive approach in the study of nature. Though his "scientific" approach is now seen as independent of religion, Bacon thought of himself as "offering a genuinely Christian approach to nature, in comparison to the preceding approaches that were understood to have been contaminated by pagan philosophy."[1] In other words, Bacon recognized that much of "natural philosophy" had non-Christian roots even if it sought to relate its philosophy to some kind of deity or to one ultimate force. Bacon tried to rid natural philosophy of those roots and see its task in light of Christianity.

Robert Boyle (1627–1691), thought to be one of the founders of modern chemistry, argued that "science" could make no progress as long as it was done with atheistic assumptions. Instead, according to him, "the universe cannot be the 'result of chance and a tumultuous concourse of atoms.'" It was God's providence alone that guarantees progress in science since that providence is given in "the constancy [and] regular and rapid motions of celestial bodies."[2] For Boyle, natural philosophy was possible only when and if it was linked to a God who caused and controls all things and whose faithful control of the world provided for a consistency in the universe. That consistency was necessary if there was going to be true scientific progress.

Isaac Newton (1642–1726), who was one of the most influential thinkers in Western history, is today known as a brilliant scientist. In his day, he was known as a natural philosopher. He made substantial contributions to areas such as laws of motion and of gravitation. Even so, and perhaps surprisingly for us "moderns," Newton recognized that his task was dependent on the character and activity of God. One of Newton's bedrock beliefs was that his work had to acknowledge that "God, Providence, and therefore theology [was] central to any proper understanding of science and nature."[3] Here was a man of great stature in the discipline of science who would likely not recognize some of what passes for science today.

We can see in these examples that the modern, common understanding of the relationship of science to Christianity is *not* normal. Since the consensus, historically, has been that Christianity and science are compatible and are meant to go together, why do so many now believe there is a conflict?

This notion of a conflict between Christianity and science can be traced, generally, to the Enlightenment. The Enlightenment, which was developing during the days of Boyle and Newton, was an era in which the thinkers of the day began to challenge all external authority. The problem with challenging all authority is that the one challenging becomes the ultimate authority. The Enlightenment era is also called the Age of Reason because it sought to ground all truth in individual thinking. Truth could not have its source in a religion or a creed. Religions were hostile to unshackled truth. Real truth had to be found in the proper and unfettered use of reason.

It would be impossible to overstate the significance of the Enlightenment on the years that followed, even up to the present day. We've all grown up breathing Enlightenment air. Many of us know of no other way to think than in the terms the Enlightenment set forth. Its influence is profound, deep, and nearly universal.

It was in this Enlightenment context that the idea of a conflict between science and Christianity began. This "conflict" was promoted in earnest in the mid-nineteenth century by two Americans, John William Draper (1812–1882) and Andrew Dickson White (1832–1918). Their writings stressed the "conflict," or "warfare," between Christianity and science. Draper was upset by proclamations from the Roman Catholic Church that declared the pope to be infallible (when he spoke "officially") and elevated revealed doctrine above the human sciences. His quarrel was almost exclusively with Roman Catholicism. The Vatican's hands were, he said, "steeped in blood."[4] His book, *History of the Conflict*

Between Religion and Science (1874), went through at least fifty printings and ten translations. It was by far the most influential book of the period.

White's *A History of the Warfare of Science with Theology in Christendom* (1896) also went through numerous editions and was translated into four other languages. White saw the authoritarianism of theology as destructive of science, and he used militaristic language to denounce it. In a recent republication of that work, Tom Flynn, in his introduction, writes, "Insofar as science and religion came to be viewed as enemies, with science holding the moral high ground—and insofar as that conviction contributed to the growth of rationalism, naturalism and secularism across the West during the twentieth century—Andrew Dickson White stands, however inadvertently, as one of the most effective and influential advocates for unbelief."[5]

As almost anyone will recognize, however, the popularity of the "science against Christianity" notion is not simply a product of these two highly influential books. The single most important influence was another book, *The Origin of the Species*. Written by Charles Darwin and published in 1859, the views set forth in this book were the gasoline that was poured on the already raging fire of the Enlightenment.

Once Darwin's view of evolution was set forth and propagated, the conflict between Christianity and science was inevitable. The soil in which Darwin's ideas were planted had already been made abundantly rich and fertile by the Enlightenment. If human reason was the foundation of all truth, then surely any view that can explain the beginning of life without need of God, or of his authority, fits in perfectly.

In the history of science, Darwin's view is new, but it is not, from a historical perspective, normal. The norm in the history of science was to see nature as understandable only within the context of nature's God. But Darwin's view didn't need God. And, as we will see next, with Darwin's views, the newer view is not the better one.

Foundational

In the modern period, there has been a concerted and, to some extent, successful effort to divorce science from religion, especially from Christianity. As we noted, that effort moved with lightning speed after the introduction of the theory of evolution.

The subject of evolution could occupy volumes. We will be brief in our discussion. There were evolutionary theories prior to Darwin and many that developed since Darwin. As a general rule, when the term "evolution" is used, it almost always includes the idea of an unguided process of species development and change. There are theories of evolution that are "theistic." They suppose that a god guided the process from the beginning. For the vast majority of people, however, "evolution" means an unguided process of biological development.

Without question, evolution has become the dominant concept in biology and other like sciences. Not only is it dominant, but for some it is the only respectable position to hold. Remember what we said in chapter 2. The noted scientist Richard Dawkins, in his enthusiastic support of evolution, said, "It is absolutely safe to say that if you meet somebody who claims not to believe in evolution, that person is ignorant, stupid or insane (or wicked, but I'd rather not consider that)."[6]

The title of this chapter recognizes the pressure that statements like Dawkins's exert on Christian belief. Though Dawkins may be speaking in hyperbole, Christians recognize that to say you don't believe in evolution is like saying you don't believe in air and sunshine. Such a statement will normally produce, for those who hear it, either pity or vitriol. You will be looked at as either naïve or ignorant. How could someone not believe in evolution in the twenty-first century?

There are a multitude of answers to that question, but we should recognize a couple of things in response. First, the theory of evolution itself has gone through numerous changes and mutations since its ascendancy in the last hundred years. The theory of evolution is actually numerous theories of evolution, each one attempting to explain how life can begin from something that is nonliving. Second, the main reason that Darwin's theory caught on and developed is not, in the first place, because it was a completely new and previously never conceived theory. Ideas like Darwin's can be traced back thousands of years to ancient Greece.

Instead, the main reason Darwin's ideas were affirmed and promoted is because they were planted in the soil of the Enlightenment. Since the Enlightenment was intent on abolishing all external authority and was wanting to find the answers to life's questions by way of human reasoning and experimentation alone, evolution was the significant hinge that allowed the Enlightenment door to swing open as wide as possible. With a theory of evolution in place, we could all now affirm that from the beginning to the end of life, we are in no need of a god. The world, as a matter of fact, runs on its own steam and is not a product of any causing and controlling deity.

But there is a problem with this Enlightenment/evolution view. The problem is not its popularity; that much is certain. Dawkins's statement shows how strongly people hold to some view of evolution. The problem is that the theory is utterly incoherent.

The incoherence is this. Someone who believes that evolution is a random and chance-produced process believes also that the universe is only natural (not in any way supernatural) and only made up of matter, or "material" (nothing immaterial or spiritual can exist). Everything that we believe, on this view, is produced somehow by the material that makes up a human being. All of our beliefs are a product of the matter that composes our bodies.

Now let's suppose this is true: Everything we believe is produced only by the material of our bodies. Then the question to ask is, How can we have any guarantee that our beliefs are true? Certainly, what we believe might help us in adapting to our environment, and evolution loves the notion of adaptability. But whether our beliefs are true cannot be determined simply through the material workings of our brains and bodies. What our brains produce would be no more than the random production of bubbles in a carbonated drink. In each case, the outcome is simply a product of the material that has been randomly put together and produced in us.

Belief in unguided evolution that some cling to so tightly is itself a product of a random collection of bodily materials. It has no more to commend it than the random, chemical production of carbonated bubbles. It may provide a way for us to affirm life without God, but it cannot provide a way for us to affirm that anything we believe is true. Though the theory of evolution is embraced, inculcated, and celebrated by so many, the reality is that it has no foundation. It has no way to make sense of its own theory. And a theory that cannot make sense of itself is, by definition, incoherent. To have no foundation is not simply an academic problem; it is a problem that goes to the very heart of what is true and why it is true.

I can illustrate the problem of a lack of foundation this way. I was speaking one evening to a group of university students about the Bible and about God's revelation in all of creation. After the meeting was over, I went to the back of the room to get some coffee. A man came up to me and introduced himself as one of the professors of physics at the university. He also told me that he was an atheist. But then he said something that was remarkable. He said, "What struck me about your talk is that as I teach physics as an atheist, I have no way to affirm or argue why the laws of physics are the way they are. All I can teach are the laws." This man recognized that even though he was an accomplished physicist, he had no way, no foundation, that could guarantee him that the laws *were* laws and that the world would continue to run in a regular and predictable pattern. All he could do was state the laws.

This is why the theory of unguided evolution cannot have a solid ground. People have, for thousands of years, recognized that the world, the universe, needs some kind of organizing and unifying principle if we are going to study it and affirm its laws and its potential. Without such a principle, all we have is a random series of events that just happen to produce something we now call human beings. Only an Enlightenment mentality could embrace and promote the idea of unguided evolution. Any theory that is based only on the natural and the material will never be able to make sense of the world. No matter how loudly it shouts, "This is true!" there remains no place to stand. It is shouting into the void.

In the history of science, the recognition of a unifying principle of nature found its true home in Christianity. Christianity gives us a true beginning point, a *genesis*, for a proper understanding of human life. In Christianity we find out that God created human beings in a singularly unique way, by breathing in the breath of life. That in-breathing distinguished human beings from everything else in God's creation. It also embedded human beings firmly in God's creation as those who were meant to oversee and tend the rest of what God had made (Gen. 1:28–30).

Given the historical novelty of modern science, together with the incoherence of evolutionary theories, the real question to ask is not why someone would believe Christianity in the face of modern science, but why someone would believe modern science in the face of Christianity. The answer is all too obvious. The Enlightenment was not an argument that human beings were self-sufficient; it was a declaration that they wanted to be. Modern science has done nothing to discredit the truths of Christianity; it has simply dismissed them.

As we have seen, Richard Dawkins provides a clear example of this kind of declaration. In his book *The God Delusion*, he says this: "The God of the Old Testament is arguably the most unpleasant character in all of fiction. Jealous and proud of it; a petty, unjust unforgiving control-freak; a vindictive, bloodthirsty ethnic-cleanser; a misogynistic homophobic racist, infanticidal, genocidal, filicidal, pestilential, megalomaniacal, sadomasochistic, capriciously malevolent bully."[7] This is not a statement of open-minded and "scientific" curiosity, nor is it a statement of "scientific" objectivity.

Anyone who thinks as Dawkins does, or in similar ways, will be all too happy to embrace a theory that leaves such a God completely out of the universe. The problem is that for Dawkins, any pettiness, any unjust, unforgiving, vindictive, misogynistic, homophobic, racist, infanticidal, genocidal behavior on the part of any person, anywhere, at any time, can only be a product of their material and natural makeup. If that is true, then these characteristics are no more important or morally repulsive than randomly produced carbonated bubbles. It is difficult to see, on Dawkins's own theory, why any of these kinds of materially produced behaviors are a problem.

Belief in Christianity, unlike belief in unguided evolution, has a foundation. Its foundation is what God has said, first in his Word and also in his world. With that foundation, science can be grounded. Without it, there is no place left for the scientist to stand. He is unable to produce the coherence needed for science to thrive.

Responses

One of the objections that comes to those who oppose evolution is that the fossil record clearly reveals that there were evolutionary changes in species. There are at least two responses to this objection. First, Darwin himself recognized that the fossil record was actually an evidential argument against evolution. According to Darwin, "Geology assuredly does not reveal any such finely-graduated organic chain; and this, perhaps, is the most obvious and serious objection which can be urged against the theory."[8] In other words, if evolution is true, the fossil record should have an abundance not just of changes within species but of intermediate species, that is, species that are "between" a bird and a reptile, for example, or between a monkey and a human. But there are none.

Because of this problem, some scientists proposed the idea of "punctuated equilibrium." This theory assumes that evolution might have happened rapidly, rather than over long periods of time. It happened so quickly that there would be few, if any, fossil records of intermediate species. It is not difficult to see that this theory was developed in light of the reality of no fossil record of intermediate species, not because there was any scientific evidence for some kind of rapid evolution.

The second response that we could give to those who would propose the fossil record as evidence of evolution is that the record itself assumes a certain progression of history in order to determine various dates and stages in history. The dating of history and its stages in evolutionary theories assume that things happened in the past in the same way, generally speaking, as they happen now. History, they assume, has been uniform in the way it has proceeded through time. There is no evidence for this kind of uniformity; it is simply assumed.

For those of us who believe what Scripture says, we recognize that God initiated a cataclysmic event in history—a universal flood. Given the flood, we simply cannot assume that history has been uniform in the development of fossils and other evidence. As we said, the assumption of the uniformity of history is only an assumption; there is no evidence for it. The notion of a universal flood is given in Scripture; it is not merely blind assumption. Given the havoc that such a flood would wreak on the world, the actual dating of fossils and other evidence would include such an event.

Another well-worn response to those who oppose evolution in favor of Christianity is that Christians just blindly assume their position, while evolution is based on scientific evidence.

We should be far enough along in this book by now to antici-pate how a Christian might respond to this objection. For example, at the beginning of the book the insightful quote from C. S. Lewis,

"I believe in Christianity as I believe that the sun has risen: not only because I see it, but because by it I see everything else."

Christians do not blindly believe. Their belief has both personal and universal application. Personally, as Lewis says, we believe Christianity because we see it. We see it in Scripture, we see it in the church, we see it in our friends and in ourselves. Christianity is not just a set of propositions that we affirm. It is an entire life.

But it also has universal application. As Lewis says, by it we see everything else. Christianity says something about everything (for example, that everything is created and sustained by God). It doesn't say everything about everything, but it does give us all that we need in order to properly view the world and everything in it. Because Christianity gives us a foundation for everything, it is a total worldview.

As we have seen, theories of evolution are not in any way able to carry the weight that Christianity assumes to itself. You cannot say, at least not with any coherence with respect to evolution, that by it, you see everything else. Evolution cannot even account for its own theory, much less for other central and important things that we all believe. In believing only in the natural and material, it cannot account for the love between a man and a woman, for the dignity of each human being, for happiness and grief. It cannot account for most of what makes us human. Evolution is random, unguided, and without moral or ethical content. If any position is accepted with blinders on, it would have to be evolution.

When it comes to modern science, then, we cannot ascribe to some of its most basic tenets. For Christians, the "now" is not the norm, and newer is not better. We believe in Christianity because only Christianity can provide the true foundation for any science, modern or otherwise. That which calls itself "science" while divorcing itself from Christianity is lost in incoherence; it cannot be rationally believed.

Conclusion

There are volumes more that can be said about the relationship and distinction between Christianity and modern science. The material in this chapter is just a beginning. But it is an important and crucial beginning. Once we see that science has had a long and fruitful history in harmony with Christianity, and once we see that theories of evolution have no foundation to support them, we can begin to understand why Christianity is the only real option available to human beings and to scientists.

The books in the following list are just a small sample of the literature available. We have tried to list resources that can delve more deeply into the particular topics broached here.

Questions for Reflection

1. Why is it important for most who believe in evolution that it be unguided?
2. How should Christians respond to the Enlightenment view of human reason?
3. In what ways does the abundance of design in the universe refute typical views of evolution?
4. Is it possible to believe what the Bible says and to believe in evolution?

Recommended Reading

Harrison, Peter. *The Territories of Science and Religion*. Chicago: University of Chicago Press, 2015.

Meyer, Stephen C. *Darwin's Doubt: The Explosive Origin of Animal Life and the Case for Intelligent Design*. Reprint edition. New York: HarperOne, 2014.

Poythress, Vern Sheridan. *Redeeming Science: A God-Centered Approach*. Wheaton, IL: Crossway, 2006.

CHAPTER 9

WHY BELIEVE IN GOD DESPITE THE EVIL IN THE WORLD?

In one sense, the so-called "problem of evil" has been evident in almost every chapter of this book. Whenever we begin to think about why we believe something, we inevitably begin to look at problems and errors and all sorts of things that remind us that this world is not perfect. Not only is it not perfect, but we would be hard-pressed to point to anything that is not affected by imperfections and deficiencies. Because of the omnipresence of evil in the world, anyone who considers the issue recognizes immediately what evil is. We all experience it. Everyone we know experiences it. The world itself, with its natural disasters and catastrophes, is as much the subject of the problem of evil as human beings are. There is no question that evil is a problem. But just what, exactly, is the problem?

We have already looked at the problem of sin in chapter 5. There we saw sin in the context of the salvation that is available to us in Jesus Christ. In this chapter, it is important to recognize that even though we will stay with the more typical terminology of the problem of evil, the problem itself is just another way of thinking about the problem of sin. In other words, "evil" and "sin" are two words that mean the same thing.

At the outset, we have to confess that the problem of evil is perhaps the most perplexing problem that Christians face. There are a number of reasons for its perplexity, which we will discuss. First, though, we will give a famous example of how the tension between the existence of evil and the existence of God has been discussed.

The late British philosopher Antony Flew told a now-famous parable of "The Invisible Gardener." Two explorers find a garden in the middle of a jungle. In this garden are many flowers and not many weeds. One explorer believes there must be a Gardener who tends the plot—how else could the garden be so orderly and well-kept? The other explorer refuses to believe that there is a Gardener. They decide to stay a while and watch to see if a Gardener comes. They wait and wait, but nothing happens. The believing explorer still affirms his belief in a Gardener. Since they have seen no evidence of a Gardener, he suggests that the Gardener is, perhaps, invisible.

The two explorers agree to wait longer. They set up an electrified barbed-wire fence and patrol it with bloodhounds in case the invisible Gardener might be tangible or detectable in some way. They continue to wait, but still nothing happens. The wires never sway, and the bloodhounds never bark. The believer continues to maintain his belief in existence of the Gardener. But now he has to qualify his belief again. He says the Gardener is not only invisible, but he is also intangible and insensitive to electric shock. He has no scent and makes no sound, so cannot be detected by the dogs. Yet, he says, this Gardener continues to care for and tend the garden. Finally, the explorer who doesn't believe in the existence of the Gardener despairs and asks the believer, "Tell me this: What's the difference between an invisible, intangible, undetectable Gardener and no Gardener at all?"

The point Flew is trying to make with this parable is that whenever people who believe in God encounter a problem that would question that belief, they always respond with some qualification of their God that allows them to keep believing.

There are at least two aspects to Flew's story. The first is the philosophical aspect. Flew was attempting to illustrate that any statement that cannot be, at least possibly, falsified, has to be nonsense. His claim is that any statement that has endless qualifications to it, in the end, means nothing. For a statement to be meaningful, Flew argued, if you can't posit some situation that could, possibly, render a statement false, it cannot be meaningful. This aspect of Flew's discussion can be quite technical, but fortunately we don't need to pursue it here. Its implications for Christians is that unless we can propose a situation in which God does not exist, then our Christianity is meaningless.

The second aspect to Flew's parable is the one that relates more directly to our topic in this chapter. Here is what Flew says after telling the parable: "Someone tells us that God loves us as a father loves his children. We are reassured. But then we see a child dying. His Heavenly Father reveals no obvious sign of concern. Some qualification is made. Just what would have to happen to entitle us to say 'God does not love us' or even 'God does not exist'? What would have to occur to constitute for you a disproof of the love of, or of the existence of, God?"[1] Flew's conclusion was that, for Christians, there is nothing that could be said that would disprove the existence of God. For that reason, he thought, the God of Christianity is dead; he has "died the death of a thousand qualifications." In other words, Christians find an excuse for every problem that is presented to them, so that, in the end, the God of Christianity makes no difference in the world. If he existed at all, he would be invisible, intangible, undetectable, and, therefore, of no use at all.

The important point for us to notice is that the example Flew uses in his complaint is the death of a child. Even in such horrendous circumstances, says Flew, the "Heavenly Father reveals no sign of concern."[2] In other words, it was the problem of suffering and evil that motivated Flew's conclusion that God must be dead.

The Problem

The Greek philosopher Epicurus (341–271 BC), whose followers—Epicureans—continued into the period of the New Testament (see Acts 17:18), defined the problem of evil in a series of questions about God and his character: "Is he willing to prevent evil, but not able? then he is impotent. Is he able, but not willing? then he is malevolent. Is he both able and willing? whence then is evil?"[3] There are a couple of aspects to this problem that Epicurus mentions that we need to highlight.

First, the problem of evil is a problem for Christians. It is a problem that arises because of our belief in God and because of the character of the God we believe in.

As we noted in chapter 2, those who do not believe in God have a completely different problem when "evil" is discussed. Even though they continue to want to make statements and declarations about what is right and wrong, they really have no way of explaining what evil is. In order for evil to be evil, it must be contrasted with something or someone that is wholly good.

Atheists, agnostics, and those who will not acknowledge God have no standard that allows them to define, by contrast, what evil is. So we have to recognize that there are two "kinds" of problems when we think about evil. We will be concerned in this chapter with the Christian problem.

The second thing that Epicurus brings out in the quotation is that the problem of evil is a problem because of some of the most basic characteristics that Christians affirm about God. So, the problem of evil is shown in these two statements:

1. God is omnipotent, omniscient, and wholly good.
2. There is a vast amount of evil in the world.

According to these two statements, when we consider these three characteristics of God, the fact that there is so much evil in the world seems incoherent. There is a basic and obvious incompatibility between the existence of this God and the amount of evil in the world. Like oil and water, there seems to be no way to "mix" these two facts together.

As we think about the problem of evil, we are thinking about one of the biggest issues that Christians face. Philosophers through the ages have seen this problem as the "Achilles' heel" of Christianity. It is the one problem that brings the entire Christian faith down.

But the problem is not only a philosophical problem. It is a deeply personal and pastoral problem. All of us have been personally affected by sin and evil. We face it every day of our existence. It is a problem that every church and every pastor experiences. There are serious consequences in the church because of the presence of evil that exists, even in Christians. How do we respond to this multi-faceted issue?

The more obvious "solutions" to this problem create bigger problems for Christians. One solution might be to deny one of the characteristics of God given in the first statement. So if we decide that God is not omnipotent, then he would not have the power to stop evil. We could then understand why evil permeates the world. God is not able to stop it.

Or if we could say that God is not omniscient, then he would not have known what we would do when he created us; he could not have known that we would bring evil into the world. Since God couldn't have known we would commit evil, we can see why evil exists. God took a risk in creating us.

Or, finally, we could say that God is not wholly good, and then evil would reflect something of his character. Maybe God is both good and evil, and the world shows us both aspects of his character.

None of these options has been seriously put forth by orthodox Christians. Down through the centuries, these three characteristics of God—his omnipotence, his omniscience, and his goodness— have been affirmed by every Christian who recognizes what Scripture says about God. To deny any of these three attributes of God is to deny God himself.

The complaint from people like Flew, and many others who see the incompatibility of God's existence and the existence of so much evil, is that it is unwise, even downright irrational, to continue to believe something when there is such strong evidence that either undercuts or rebuts its truth. So, Christians are told, it is unwise and downright irrational to believe in the kind of God you believe in when all around us, and in the world, is such a massive amount of evidence to the contrary—evidence that shows that your belief in God is not logical. The Christian's only alternative, we're told, is to give up that belief.

Whatever we think of Flew's parable of the Invisible Gardener, we can all relate to the motivation behind the parable. The motivation behind the parable is the sometimes horrendous affliction that comes to us and is obvious to anyone whose eyes are open. The difficulty with such atrocities is that they continue to happen, and happen with nauseating regularity, in the face of our insistence that God, who is goodness itself, exists.

How should Christians respond to this problem? Why believe in this kind of God when there is so much evil in the world?

Reasons

Instead of denying the truth of God's existence in the face of evil, Christians have developed responses to the challenge. For Christians, the question might be put this way: What might be the reasons for the existence of evil, given the truth of God's existence?

For many who deny the existence of God in the face of so much evil, the challenge is often put this way: You Christians need to give a God-justifying reason for the presence of evil. You need to tell us how this kind of God you believe in is justified in his actions, given the universal presence of evil. Why think that there has to be a "God-justifying" reason for evil?

In the eighteenth century, a philosopher by the name of Gottfried Wilhelm von Leibniz (1646–1716) wrote a work titled *Theodicy*. The word theodicy is a combination of two Greek words. The first, *Theos*, means God; the second, *dike*, means justify. Whenever the subject of "theodicy" comes up, we are asking what reasons, or justification, God would have in creating a world that contains so much evil.

Christian motivation for a "theodicy" is not always wrong. Even the most pious Christians, in their honest moments, recognize the need for some kind of response to the universal and pervasive presence of evil. We are interested in a reason not because we want to know everything, or because we think God owes us an explanation, but because we know that the evil in the world just doesn't fit with everything else that we know about God and his character. Christians want to be able to defend their belief in God's existence, and we want that defense to be grounded in what God himself says about it.

One of the answers that has been given to the problem of theodicy is called the "Greater Good Defense." There are different versions of this defense, but all of them try to show that evil exists so that other virtues could exist and be apparent. The Greater Good Defense asks, How could there be virtue unless there was vice? How could there be courage without danger? How could all things work for good unless there is evil to overcome? Like a child who has to endure the pain of a shot, the shot is for the greater good of health for the child in the face of disease.

The problem with this defense is that it still leaves so much evil and suffering unexplained and apparently senseless. What "greater good" is there in a random killing, or mass torture, or, as Flew points out, a child's death? Doesn't the Christian view of God recognize that he is holy and good, without any evil at all? Doesn't this show that goodness, virtue, and holiness can exist, as they do in God, without the presence of evil? And wasn't the Garden of Eden proclaimed by God to be "very good" when there was no evil present in it? The notion that there needs to be evil for there to be a "greater good" doesn't ring true, given other things Christians believe.

One of the most famous responses to the problem of evil was

given by the church father Augustine (354–430 AD). A quick summary of Augustine's life is needed to see the background that motivated his response.

Before his conversion to Christianity, Augustine adopted a number of different philosophies to try to explain the meaning of life. One of those philosophies was called "Manicheanism." Manicheanism began in the third century AD. One of its primary teachings was that reality was ultimately dualistic. That means that there exist two ultimates, an ultimate good and an ultimate evil; the two coexist together. For Augustine, before his conversion, this was the solution to the problem of evil. The reason the world consists of both good and evil is because the nature of ultimate reality consists of these dual powers.

When Augustine was converted, he realized that he could no longer hold to an ultimate dualism in reality. Reality is ultimately *good* because God, who is ultimate, is only good and there is no evil in him. Augustine began, as a Christian, to seek to find a way to "justify" God, given the fact of so much evil in the world.

As a Christian, Augustine knew that God created all things and that everything he created was good (see Gen. 1:4, 10, 12, 18, 21, 31). Did God create evil as well?

Augustine answered no to this question. It is true that God created everything. But, says, Augustine, we have to recognize that evil is not a thing! Instead, it is a lack, or a denial, of a thing. The Latin term for Augustine's view is that evil is a *privatio boni*, which means a privation, or lack, of the good.

This may all sound too abstract, but it can be illustrated fairly simply. When we speak of something being "immoral," what we mean to express by that word is that something lacks, or denies, the moral. In that way it goes against, or contradicts, what is moral. Something immoral is a denial of morality.

The reason Augustine saw this as a fitting explanation of evil in the world is because if evil is a lack or denial of what is good, it is not a thing at all. It is, instead, a lack or denial of a thing. Evil, then, is not something God created, because it is not a thing. It is the lack of a thing.

Not only is evil not a thing, but it is completely dependent on goodness in order to be what it is; it is parasitic on the good. The notion of "immorality" makes no sense unless there is morality. But the opposite is not true. Morality does not depend on immorality for its definition. Evil's characteristics, according to Augustine (and many others in the church have taught this as well), are that it is not a thing, but a denial of the good, and it could not be what it is without the good first being what it is.

This view includes some basic Christian truths. Since God is only good and is ultimate, it is true that evil depends on the good (on God) to be what it is. And it is true that evil can be defined as anything that goes against, or denies, God's character. In that sense, Augustine's view expresses some Christian truth.

But there are problems that come with this view. Even if Augustine's view helps to explain something about the nature of evil—as a denial of God's character and as something dependent on God—it does not go very far in explaining why evil was introduced into the world in the first place. In other words, even if evil is a lack or a denial of goodness, we still haven't answered the question of why so much evil is in the world. To repeat a point, God himself is not evil— there is no lack in him and he cannot deny his own character—so there still seems to be no reason for evil to be present in our world.

Another problem is that defining evil as a lack or denial doesn't do justice to the real power of evil to destroy, twist, and pervert reality. Something that is only a lack would not have such destructive power. Clearly, evil, if it is a lack, is an extremely powerful lack. Augustine's view contains some basic Christian truths, but still does not get to the "Why evil?" question.

Another response to the problem of evil—one of the most popular answers given to the problem of evil—is that God created man with "free will." By "free will" is meant that our choices to obey or disobey could in no way be controlled, ordained, or designed by God. "Free" in this sense means "completely free of God's control."

It will be easy to see why this is a popular option. It "justifies" God because it "releases" him from any connection with the decisions human beings make. The decisions we make are completely our decisions, and there is no way that God could have any control over those decisions. Thus, we are completely responsible for evil because our choices were within only our control.

There are serious problems with this view. One problem is that it contradicts what Scripture teaches about God's control. Proverbs 16:33, for example, says, "The lot is cast into the lap, but its every decision is from the Lord." Daniel 4:35 extols God's complete control: "All the peoples of the earth are regarded as nothing. He does as he pleases with the powers of heaven and the peoples of the earth. No one can hold back his hand or say to him: 'What have you done?'" The apostle Paul, in a concise and comprehensive way, affirms that God "works out everything in conformity with the purpose of his will" (Eph. 1:11). A multitude of other passages could be listed here. The conclusion to these passages is that God has never, because he could not, relinquished control over that which he has made. In that sense, there is no "free" will, if by "free" we mean that there is no way God could have any control over it.

If it were true that human beings could make choices that were independent of God and his control, then God is "off the hook" for the presence of evil in the world. This option is, at root, a denial of God's omniscience, or his omnipotence, in order to explain evil. It might deny God's omniscience because even though God knows everything that could be known, he cannot know the future, since it does not yet exist. The future can be known by no one, not even God. Or, it might deny God's omnipotence by asserting that because God made us "free," he chose not to retain any power over our decisions. In either case, God is now "justified" for evil's existence.

The problem with this "justification" of God is that the price is too high. In effect, it reduces God down to a human level, not able to know all things or not controlling everything. To explain evil by diminishing God and his glory should not be a Christian option. God is sovereign.

So if God is in control of even the evil in the world, then it looks as though we have made no progress in "justifying" him. This brings us back to the original question: How should we think of God—who is working out "everything in conformity with the purpose of his will"—in light of so much evil in the world?

Biblical Reasons

The reasons given by some for the existence of God and of evil, even though they might contain elements of truth, do not provide what they hope to. They might provide a little nugget of insight here and there, but they don't really address the problem between the incompatibility that we see in the existence of God and the presence of evil.

In the end, the only way to provide an explanation for this incompatibility is to see what the Bible can tell us about it. When we recognize the Bible as our only help in addressing this issue, we also recognize that since the Bible is God's Word, we have a completely trustworthy source available to us.

When this issue is discussed, especially in philosophical circles, it is sometimes said that appealing to the Bible is illegitimate, since the parties in the discussion might not believe the Bible. So we must be able to address the conundrum without appealing to Scripture.

There are various ways to respond to this objection. In any response to such an objection, two points are primary. First, we have to remember that the problem we're discussing is a specifically Christian problem. It is a problem that those who believe in God have because it is a problem of incompatibility. If one believes there is no God, then there is no incompatibility (we have to remember, though, that other, more serious, problems plague atheism's attempt to explain evil).

The second point, related to the first, is that whenever we affirm certain characteristics or attributes of God, the question of the source of that affirmation should be addressed. So, because part of the incompatibility includes the fact that God is omnipotent, omniscient, and wholly good, we need to be clear that such attributes of God can be known of him only because of what he has said about himself. In other words, this description of God is a revealed description. So it follows that we should see what else God's revelation can tell us about this issue.

There are three central teachings of the Bible that are needed to frame a response to this problem. Only when these three teachings provide the framework can we see the picture clearly.

1. God

The first central teaching that informs our understanding is the Bible's teaching about God and his activity in initiating and sustaining all of creation. The initiation of creation actually began in eternity, before the world and time even existed. The Lord says,

> I make known the end from the beginning, from ancient times, what is still to come. I say, "My purpose will stand, and I will do all that I please. From the east I summon a bird of prey; from a far-off land, a man to fulfill my purpose. What I have said, that I will bring about; what I have planned, that I will do" (Isa. 46:10–11).

This passage, and others like it, has to do with God's decree. The decree of God is the initiation of creation. Father, Son, and Holy Spirit determined, in eternity, the "end from the beginning." They decided every aspect of creation.

When the apostle Paul is referring to this decree, which includes the salvation that the Lord's people will receive, he says this:

> Praise be to the God and Father of our Lord Jesus Christ, who has blessed us in the heavenly realms with every spiritual blessing in Christ. For he chose us in him before the creation of the world to be holy and blameless in his sight. In love he predestined us for adoption to sonship through Jesus Christ, in accordance with his pleasure and will (Eph. 1:3–5).

These words from the apostle give us initial clues in addressing the problem of evil. Notice that Paul says that the Father chose people "in him," meaning in Christ, and that he did that "before the creation of the world." Those two words—in Christ—point to the fact that, before the creation of the world, God had already decreed a way to deal with sin and evil in the world. The reason that Jesus Christ came, in other words, was to rectify the problem that we brought into his good creation.

The first central truth that we recognize is that the problem of evil, rather than being a surprise to God or something that caused God to "adjust" his plan for creation, was recognized by God even before creation existed. It was all a part of his sovereign decree, a decree which includes the coming of the Son of God himself.

2. Image of God

The second central biblical truth is that human beings are created as image of God. As soon as God determines, by way of his own triune decree, to create man (male and female), he assigns dominion to him.

> Then God said, "Let us make mankind in our image, in our likeness, so that they may rule over the fish in the sea and the birds in the sky, over the livestock and all the wild animals, and over all the creatures that move along the ground" (Gen. 1:26).

In the six days of God's creating activity, no other created thing is given this privilege. No other created thing is meant to "image" God. Part of that image means that God creates mankind to be a "little lord" over the Lord's own house. Mankind is to take what God has made and (under God) be ruler over it, to do it good, and to use it for the good of all people.

This "dominion" command of God to mankind changes the

structure of creation entirely. For five days, creation was God's alone, to use and to organize as he saw fit. But now, on the sixth and crowning day of creation, God makes something that is meant to "image" his character, and he gives to mankind the responsibility to rule over creation. We are given no exact details as to what that rule would look like. We are not privy to the everyday activity of Adam and Eve in the Garden. But whatever they were doing, they were doing it in the context of their responsibility to God.

Clearly, then, at the initial act of creation, to be "image of God" meant that mankind—male and female (Gen. 1:27)—was in a responsible relationship to God, with responsibility that included dominion over what God had made. In one sense, God gave his creation over to mankind so that God's enjoyment of it would include the daily work and process of man's obedient dominion over it. That dominion had consequences.

We can see one of those consequences in the relationship of God to Adam in naming the animals. And because this naming process was a responsibility given by God, God's sovereignty over Adam's responsibility was highlighted; it was God who brought the animals to Adam to name (Gen. 2:19–20). It is not simply that Adam was given responsibility to name the animals. Rather, Adam was to exercise his dominion over the earth by naming the animals that God brought to him. This is a picture of God giving Adam his dominion responsibilities, even while those responsibilities are carried out in relationship to, and within the ultimate control of, the sovereign Lord God.

God not only shows his sovereignty by bringing Adam animals to name, but he shows his sovereign rule over creation as well by defining one aspect of creation that Adam and Eve could not rule or control. He set aside one tree in all of the Garden and made it clear that it was not a part of their dominion. In doing so, he was reminding them of whose creation it was in the first place.

There was, as far as we're told, nothing significant about the tree that God set apart. According to the account in Genesis, God simply designated one tree as "the tree of the knowledge of good and evil" (Gen. 2:17) and told Adam and Eve that their dominion was restricted by that tree. It was God's sovereign dominion that defined and designated the dominion of Adam and Eve.

Even as they ruled in the Garden, their rule was never meant to be exhaustive; they were not to touch, much less to rule over, that one tree. This was a visible, tangible way that God reminded Adam and Eve that their lordship over creation had its origin and its character in the ultimate Lord of all.

The rest, as they say, is history. We know all too well what happens next. Adam and Eve sinned; they were deceived into thinking that their dominion should extend to every part of the Garden, even the tree God had forbidden them to eat from. They reject God's rule and eat fruit from the tree. When they do, their relationship with God is forever changed, and God's good creation itself begins to groan (see Rom 8:19–22). Mankind falls from its sinless state, and creation loses its "goodness." Since that first sin, people have continued to attempt to be sovereign over their own lives, with nothing but tragic results. Consequences follow from the choices people make.

In other words, with the biblical picture of God's creating activity in view, we now see *both* that God is and remains sovereign—there is no indication here (or anywhere else in Scripture) that God's omnipotence or omniscience is absent—*and* that Adam and Eve's actions with respect to God's commands will have consequences for them and for the rest of creation. Adam and Eve, and everyone after them, fall from their perfect fellowship with God. When they fall, creation itself falls as well. All of creation, including especially God's created "image," is now, because of Adam and Eve's disobedience, immersed in the effects of sin. Their disobedience brought rot and ruin to an otherwise unstained creation.

These two aspects of biblical teaching help us to properly see and discuss the problem of evil. Now we recognize that everything that happens in the world was initiated by God in eternity past. Even the remedy for the problem was guaranteed before creation ever was. We also see that, even as it was all planned by God, part of God's sovereign plan was that those made in his image would be responsible agents in God's world. This is why, when Adam and Eve sinned, God judged them for their disobedience (Gen. 3:11–19). That judgment placed the blame for sin squarely on the shoulders of those who disobeyed. When Adam and Eve, as image of God, sin, their sin brings real consequences, both to themselves as well as to the rest of creation.

3. God with Us

The third central biblical truth that addresses the problem of evil is the most important of the three. It is the most important because it helps us to recognize that God sees the incompatibility of his character and evil as a serious problem. So serious is the problem that God determines to deal with it in a way that deeply involves him.

It is sometimes supposed, especially when the problem of evil is discussed, that God is "outside" the problem, perhaps aloof and unconcerned as he sits in his heavenly repose. Fortunately, this is as far from the biblical picture of God as it could be.

God is not "outside" the problem that Adam and Eve brought into his world. Instead, from the beginning of evil in the world through Adam and Eve, God comes down to earth (Gen. 3:8–10).

The word theophany points to an appearance, or manifestation, of God. There are a number of different "forms" (including a temporary human form, as in Genesis 3) that God adopted in Scripture to show people who he is. In adopting these forms, he is communicating his commitment to solve the problem of evil that we brought into the world.

When we consider the problem of "theodicy," the first thing we need to recognize is the truth of "theophany," the appearance of God. The way that God has planned, from eternity past, to "justify" himself in light of the sin and evil in the world is by coming down to his creation, appearing in his creation to address and solve the problem of evil. Far from being removed and aloof from the problem, he enters into the rot and ruin of it to destroy it.

The ultimate and permanent "theophany" of God, of course, is in Jesus Christ, who is Immanuel, God with us (Isa. 7:14, Matt. 1:23). Jesus Christ, who is fully God and fully man as one person, came into this world to set right what we ruined.

The cost that Christ paid to deal with our problem of sin was high. He died. But there was an even greater price that he paid.

Before Christ went to the cross, he prayed to his Father.

> He withdrew about a stone's throw beyond them, knelt down and prayed, "Father, if you are willing, take this cup from me; yet not my will, but yours be done." An angel from heaven appeared to him and strengthened him. And being in anguish, he prayed more earnestly, and his sweat was like drops of blood falling to the ground (Luke 22:41–44).

Here we see the Son of God himself praying to his Father, with sweat like drops of blood, in anguish, that he not have to go to the cross. The anguish and sweat were not because of the physical pain that he knew he would endure at the cross. Instead, he knew that his death included the fact that the penalty that we deserve would be placed on him.

Before he dies, Jesus cries out, "My God, my God, why have you forsaken me?" (Matt. 27:46). The death of Jesus was not just another physical death. It was a death in which the only one who had never himself sinned was made sin for us (2 Cor. 5:21). This is why he cries out, and why the Father had to forsake him. It was not because he had contributed to the problem of evil, but because we had. It was because the problem could be conquered only if the penalty we should pay was paid by him.

God, in the person of his Son, comes to us to solve the horrendous problem that we started and that only he could finish.

Antony Flew's complaint is now refuted. Remember how he put it? "Someone tells us that God loves us as a father loves his children. We are reassured. But then we see a child dying. His Heavenly Father reveals no obvious sign of concern." "His Heavenly Father reveals no obvious sign of concern?" Nothing could be further from the truth. So concerned was the Father that he sent his own child to suffer and to be forsaken by him and to die. No higher or deeper sign of his concern could be imagined.

The problem of evil, which is our fault, finds its solution only when God solves it. He solves the sin problem by becoming sin so that it will one day be destroyed.

Responses

Perhaps someone will respond to our solution by complaining that it still does not tell us why God decided to create, knowing that sin and evil would follow.

It is true that God has not made us privy to all that was in his mind when he decided to create and to redeem. This is the kind of complaint that Job wanted to speak to God about.

Job was more aware of the problem of evil and suffering than most people are because he had to live it. His family and possessions were taken from him, and he was plagued with all kinds of diseases and painful maladies. He finally decided he wanted to have a discussion with God about it.

> Then the Lord spoke to Job out of the storm:
>
> "Brace yourself like a man; I will question you, and you shall answer me. Would you discredit my justice? Would you condemn me to justify yourself? Do you have an arm like God's, and can your voice thunder like his? Then adorn yourself with glory and splendor, and clothe yourself in honor and majesty" (Job 40:6–10).

When Job wanted answers about suffering and evil, God reminded him of his character. Instead of God accepting the notion that he had to justify himself before Job, he says, "Would you condemn me to justify yourself?" And then he reminds Job of God's glory and honor.

"But," someone might complain, "that still doesn't answer the why question! Why would God plan this kind of world?"

Given what we have said to this point, that question is better addressed with a more accurate focus. "Why would God, from eternity past, plan and create a world where he himself, in the person of his Son, would come and suffer and die, being forsaken by his Father on the cross, to bring rebellious human creatures to himself?" Certainly, he didn't have to do any of this. But his plan, with all of the evil and suffering included in it, includes, preeminently, the suffering and death of his Son.

And that is where the Bible requires that we stop asking the question. We stop asking because God has given us in his revelation all that we need to know about the problem. Even so, there remain, still, the "secret things" that God does not reveal.

And we stop asking because of the depth of the riches of the wisdom and knowledge of God. His judgments remain unsearchable, and his paths continue to be beyond tracing out (Rom. 11:33). We stop asking because he is God and we are not.

God has solved the problem of evil. That solution is working itself out in history until the most obvious indication of the problem—death itself (Gen. 2:16–17)—will finally be destroyed (1 Cor. 15:54–57). In the meantime—and in the midst of questions God has chosen, for now, not to answer—the proper response to the problem of evil is to trust him. Since God is God, we can place ourselves in the hands of the one who knows the end from the beginning, who through Christ has provided our deliverance from evil for eternity.

Questions for Reflection

1. Why is God's solution to the problem of evil not satisfactory for some people?
2. What do you know of how other religions deal with the problem of evil?
3. Why do you think Paul calls death the "last enemy" (1 Cor. 15:26)?

Recommended Reading

Keller, Timothy. *Walking with God through Pain and Suffering.* Reprint edition. New York: Penguin, 2015.

Piper, John. *Lessons from a Hospital Bed.* Wheaton, IL: Crossway, 2016.

Piper, John. *Suffering and the Sovereignty of God.* Wheaton, IL: Crossway, 2006.

Lewis, C. S. *The Problem of Pain.* Revised edition. New York: HarperOne, 2015.

CHAPTER 10

WHY BELIEVE IN CHRISTIANITY ALONE?

Now that we are coming to the end of our "Know Why" book, it will be necessary for us to venture into the world of ideas one last time. The question that we are seeking to address in this chapter has three primary ideas behind it that we will discuss. Christianity is not simply one more religion. It has implications that apply to all of life and the entire world. In that way, "why believe in Christianity alone" is not only a "religious" question. It is a question about religion and about everything else. We end this book where we began.

One of the most offensive teachings of Christianity is that belief and trust in Jesus Christ is the only way to eternal life. In this chapter, we want to discuss why this teaching is so offensive and how we might respond to it.

Years ago, a book that by all estimates should have remained in obscurity, wound up spending four months on the New York Times bestseller list. It was not an easy book to read. It contained abstract philosophical concepts and ancient terminology. But it was read, and read, and read by millions.

The book was *The Closing of the American Mind* by Alan Bloom (1930–1992). One of the things that grabbed the attention of so many readers was the book's opening pages. Bloom's analysis, which resonated with so many, seemed to accurately assess the current cultural mind-set. Bloom, because of his years of experience as a college professor, put his finger on a serious problem among college students, a problem that extended to the rest of the culture as well. This is a lengthy quote, but so well expressed that it needs to be set out in full. Bloom begins his book by describing what any college professor can expect of his students:

> There is one thing a professor can be absolutely certain of: almost every student entering the university believes, or says he believes, that *truth is relative.* If this belief is put to the test, one can count on the students' reaction. They will be uncomprehending. That anyone should regard the proposition as not self-evident astonishes them, as though he were calling into question 2 + 2 = 4. These are things you don't think about.
>
> The students' backgrounds are as various as America can provide. Some are religious, some atheists; some are to the Left, some to the Right; some intend to be scientists, some humanists or professionals or businessmen; some are poor, some rich. They are unified only in their relativism and in their allegiance to equality. And the two are related in a moral intention. The *relativity of truth* is not a theoretical insight but a moral postulate. . . . That it is a moral issue for students is revealed by the character of their response when challenged—a combination of disbelief and indignation. . . . The danger they have been taught to fear from absolutism is not error but intolerance.

Relativism is necessary to openness; and this is the virtue, the only virtue, which all primary education for more than fifty years has dedicated itself to inculcating. Openness . . . is the real insight of our time. The true believer is the real danger. The study of history and of culture teaches that all the world was mad in the past; men always thought they were right, and that led to wars, persecutions, slavery. . . . The point is not to correct the mistakes and really be right; rather it is not to think you are right at all. The students, of course, cannot defend their opinion. It is something with which they have been indoctrinated.[1]

There is so much packed into Bloom's analysis. His book elaborates on the problem he mentions, and he offers his own solution to the problem.[2] His analysis of the problem, however, is as simple as it is surprising. Not only do college students believe that truth is relative, but they "cannot defend their opinion." Instead, "it is something with which they have been indoctrinated."

The problem is relativism. "Relativism" means that truth is relative to the one who believes it. In other words, my truth is mine; your truth is yours. Maybe what you and I believe to be true is the same, but that really doesn't matter. Even if what I believe to be true is the opposite of what you believe to be true, that is not a problem. Truth is in the mind of the one who believes it. It has no real "touch" with the world out there or with anyone else.

Bloom's assessment many years ago continues to ring true today. Relativism is nothing new. What is new is the particular context or culture where relativism is found. Bloom wrote his book in the 1980s. Since then, a "new" cultural expression of relativism has come (though it seems to be on its way out). This new expression is called "postmodernism."

"Postmodernism" has a number of different forms and applications. Some have said that it began as an architectural idea, in which buildings were designed with no obvious symmetry or central focus in their structure. Whatever its form, postmodernism asserts a kind of "group relativism." In a postmodern world, maybe truth is not relative just to me, or to one person, but instead it is relative to a particular group. Postmodern truth was sometimes summed up in the phrase "Truth is whatever your peers will let you get away with."[3] In other words, you and your peers define what truth is.

Relativism still looms large today. As we will see, it is the "default" position that people adopt when there is nothing outside of their own minds that they are willing to trust.

But relativism is never an only child. It is always accompanied by two siblings that look strikingly similar. These three siblings have their own personalities, but they remain a very close-knit family. You rarely see one without the other two. Whenever you see relativism, you usually see it accompanied by religious pluralism and a certain form of tolerance. These three siblings are all related, and a brief explanation of the other two ideas will show us why.

The term "religious pluralism," like relativism, can be used in a number of different ways. It is not always something negative. For example, sometimes religious pluralism just means that there are different views on religion, or different kinds of religions that exist side by side in a society. This is true enough. In our increasingly global environment, it is easy to recognize that there are a number of different religions in the world.

When "religious pluralism" is coupled with relativism, however, it is not merely descriptive—affirming that there are different religions. Instead, religious pluralism means that in some way, all the different religions are true. A popular illustration of this idea is given in a Buddhist parable:

> Once upon a time a group of religious seekers from different traditions came together and began to discuss the nature of God. Offering quite different answers, they began quarreling among themselves as to who was right and who was wrong. Finally, when no hope for a reconciliation was in sight, they called in the Buddha and asked him to tell them who was right. The Buddha proceeded to tell the following story.

> There was once a king who asked his servants to bring him all the blind people in a town and an elephant. Six blind men and an elephant were soon set before him. The king instructed the blind men to feel the animal and describe the elephant. "An elephant is like a large waterpot," said the first who touched the elephant's head. "Your Majesty, he's wrong," said the second, as he touched an ear. "An elephant is like a fan." "No," insisted a third, "an elephant is like a snake," as he held his trunk. "On the contrary, you're all mistaken," said a fourth, as he held the tusks, "An elephant is like two prongs of a plow." The fifth man demurred and said, "It is quite clear that an elephant is like a pillar," as he grasped the animal's rear leg. "You're all mistaken," insisted the sixth. "An elephant is a long snake," and he held up the tail. They all began to shout at each other about their convictions of the nature of the elephant.

> After telling the story the Buddha commented, "How can you be so sure of what you cannot see. We are all like blind people in this world. We cannot see God. *Each of you may be partly right, yet none completely so.*"[4]

In the last sentence we see a good description of what religious pluralism is. It affirms all religions as partially true. More than that, religious pluralism gains some traction because its affirmation of the partial truth of all religions rests on the notion that no one can have all the truth. This is one of the things that makes religious pluralism so appealing to so many. It is obvious that no one can have all the truth. If that is true, then what options are left when it comes to religion?

The third sibling of relativism and religious pluralism is tolerance. In some ways, tolerance is nothing more than an attitude that should naturally accompany relativism and religious pluralism. It has to do with how we perceive or act toward others who disagree with us. If truth is relative, so that your truth, even if it is "group truth," is yours, and mine is mine, then I shouldn't harbor any animosity toward you. I also should recognize that you are as "right" about what you believe as I am.

When we affirm religious pluralism, any disagreements in religion have their source in the partiality of the truth that we hold. Why would we be intolerant of a blind man who senses only the elephant's tail when we, as blind people, might sense only the elephant's tusks? Once we recognize that we're all blind people trying to feel our way through life, tolerance is the most natural attitude to hold.

Reasons

How should Christians assess these three siblings? Do Christians consider themselves a part of this family of siblings? Do we see Christianity as true *only* because we believe it? Do we think that Christianity "sees" a limited part of the same elephant that Buddhism, Hinduism, Islam, and others "see"? Is tolerance a proper Christian attitude toward other "truths" and other religions?

For Christians, the answers to these questions run counter to the three siblings of relativism, religious pluralism, and tolerance. Each of these siblings needs to be discussed in the context of Christianity.

Relativism and Christianity

I remember seeing a bumper sticker on the back of a car that read, "God says it, I believe it, that settles it." There are a couple of different ways to read this bumper sticker. Are the three statements an argument for my belief, or are they an argument for God's authority?

In other words, are the statements properly understood this way: God says it and *because* I believe it, that settles it? Or should they be read this way: *Because* God says it, that settles it, and I believe it? Where we place the "because" makes all the difference. The difference is not a minor matter. It is the difference between the relative truth of Christianity, on the one hand, or Christianity as true, whether I believe it or not, on the other.

If what Allan Bloom says is still true today (and I think it is even more true), then this distinction might be difficult for us to recognize. We can explain the distinction with a question, "Is Christianity true for me, or is it true whether or not I believe it?"

The answer to this question should be obvious. The truth of Christianity is not dependent on whether or not I believe it. Christianity is true whether it is believed or not believed.

When we think of Christianity in this way, we are moving away from truth as only subjective, which is what relativism affirms, to truth as objective. Objective truth may sound abstract and difficult, but in reality it is something that everyone has to affirm.

I remember speaking to a group of college students. One student, fresh from his philosophy class, told me after my lecture that he was convinced that there was no way to know the objective world at all. When I asked him to repeat his statement, I also grabbed an object near the lectern where I was standing and pretended that I was going to toss it in his direction. He immediately reacted and moved as if he were going to catch what I pretended to toss to him. He knew the objective world after all.

When we speak of objective truth, we are referring to the world outside ourselves. We are referring to the obvious reality that every one of us has to assume in order to live. We can't even get out of bed without assuming that the bed we lay down on the night before is the same one we wake up on, that the room we were in the night before is the same room, that the house we're in is the same house, etc., etc. Whenever we assume these things, we are making judgments about objective truth. Things outside of us remain the same, and we act accordingly.

We don't typically think about these judgments that we make. They are assumed, or presupposed. They are so much a part of our daily existence that we come to expect them.

But these things we assume argue against any serious form of relativism. They demonstrate that what we believe about the world is necessary for us if we are going to live in it. They show that even if we believe that there is no objective truth, we will still assume that we will wake up in the same bed, in the same room, etc. And we will assume that when we say, "There is no objective world," there is someone out there in the objective world who hears what we say and who understands the words we are uttering. Our words have no meaning unless there is objective truth.

Christians are interested in how such a world could exist, how it could be as reliable as it is, and how it could be understood in such a (basically) uniform way. In other words, once we recognize the necessity of a basic and objective regularity to the world and the way it works, Christianity is intent to explain the rationale for such things.

Relativism is a view that cannot be lived. I don't have the option to believe that, for me, a green light means "Stop" and a red light means "Go." If I did, chaos would result and lives would be lost. In that sense, the world around us imposes its truth on us.

The question then becomes, "What is the best way to understand the world?" When we speak of the "best" way, we're referring to a way that will make sense of the kind of world we live in, including making sense of who *we* are, and of how we ought to live in this world.

There have been myriad options presented as an answer to the question of the nature of the world. It is impossible to survey, much less to know, all the options presented.

Fortunately, the options given can be adequately summarized without getting tangled up in the details of every view. In any view that attempts to answer the question of how best to understand the world, it is assumed that either there is no God (or no way to know if God exists) or that God exists.

When we consider the first option, we meet up with our now-familiar view of naturalism. We already saw in chapter 8 some of the problems of a purely naturalistic view of the world. When we think about naturalism in light of our present topic of relativism, we continue to encounter serious problems.

Let's suppose that naturalism is the truth about the world. Everything we encounter or think is just "natural." How can we make sense of any truth from a naturalistic point of view? What if I decide to be a relativist? That shouldn't be a problem to a naturalist because my decisions and my beliefs are just "natural." What if someone else thinks relativism is wrong? That too shouldn't trouble a naturalist, since that belief is natural as well.

A naturalist will respond by trying to explain why there is a certain "natural" order in the world, an order that denies any kind of crass relativism. "Look at how the geese fly," he might say. "They naturally recognize that there needs to be one who leads them, and they all fly in the same direction."

But this kind of response ignores the difficulties present in human existence. We could compare the geese, for example, to the Nazi regime under Hitler. They all flew in the same direction with their fearless leader. Is there any way a naturalist could pronounce Nazi truth, which is natural truth, worse than the natural truth that motivated those who fought against Hitler? How can naturalism escape the trap of relative truth?

The truth is that it cannot. As Dostoevsky put it so long ago in *The Brothers Karamazov*, if God does not exist, then anything is permissible.[5] Maybe a naturalist could argue that not everything is permissible. We have to learn to live together, after all. But even if individual relativism is denied for the sake of living together, there can be no way to argue against group relativism. It brings us back to the postmodern predicament.

Christians believe that truth is objective and outside of them. Christians, by definition, believe the truth that is outside of them, but they do not believe that truth has its home in their subjective belief. Instead, truth is first of all located in God himself—Father, Son, and Holy Spirit—it is not something that originates in the world around us.

The grain of truth in relativism is that truth is relative to a person. In Christianity, however, that person is the Tri-Personal God, who himself is the truth. There has to be a point where truth originates and where it finds its proper home. Without that point, there is no way for truth to be outside of us and objective.

When we recognize that truth has its proper home in God himself, then we move, once again, as we have seen throughout the book, to what God has said in order to discover what the truth tells us about the world.

God tells us, first (as we saw in chapter 6), that he is the Creator of the world. The reason there are things in the world right now is because God spoke and created them. Things exist now because he exists in and of himself. He could give existence to things because he is existence. He does not derive existence from something else.

God tells us that once he began to create, he instilled order into his creation. He created specific things on specific days. After creating on a given day, "there was evening, and there was morning" (see Gen. 1:5, 8, 13, 19, 23, 31). In other words, even while God is creating, he is establishing a certain order—what we now call "laws"—in the world.

When God decides to create mankind—male and female— something special happens. As we have already discussed, he creates by breathing into man the breath of life (Gen. 2:7). This action serves to distinguish human beings from all the other creatures on earth. In the previous five days, God created and commanded. On the sixth day, God creates, breathes into man, and then commands. This illustrates, in part, what God means when he decides that he will create something in his image (Gen. 1:26–27).

Because human beings are in God's image, we can understand why truth is something beyond us. The "responsibility" of an image is to reflect its original. An image in a mirror reflects the original that is in front of it. As creatures of God who are meant to reflect God, who is himself the truth, human beings are supposed to recognize and affirm the truth of who we are (God's image) and of what the world is (created and sustained by God).

This is the first thing that Christians should recognize when we are confronted with the relativism of so many. Truth cannot be relative. There is no way to account for it if it is. The only way to account for truth is to see it as something that is both beyond us (because it is in God himself) and is given to us (in God's revelation). That way, we can affirm objective truth and, at the same time, recognize that the truth that we have is, in the first place, not ours, but God's.

Once we see relativism as an illegitimate idea, we can begin to see as well the illegitimacy of its sibling, religious pluralism.

Religious Pluralism and Christianity

Relativism is the "big brother" of its smaller, more religious, sibling. Addressing relativism first also helps Christians speak to the issues surrounding religious pluralism.

In the Buddhist parable of the elephant, religious pluralism is a product of human limitations. It reasons that we ought to affirm that all religions are at least partly correct because we can only "see," or "sense," in a limited way. Religious pluralism recognizes the finitude of human existence. Limited knowledge requires the humility of seeing other views as equally legitimate.

It is impossible to argue against the notion that we are all limited, sometimes severely so. But there is another assumption in the elephant parable that might not be as obvious. Somehow and in some way it is determined that what each of the six men are "sensing" in their different and limited ways is an elephant. How can we know that all six men are accessing parts of an elephant and not of a rhinoceros or a hippopotamus or a house? Or, even worse, what if some are aware of an elephant, while others are aware of a hippo, or a rock, or a mountain, or . . . ? The assumption of the parable is that everyone is aware of the same thing but differently. How could we know this?

In fairness, the parable is trying to illustrate how religious people can have different views of the same God. The elephant represents the God of these various religions.

But this only increases the problem. If the elephant represents the same God, doesn't the parable begin with an assumption that is anything but clear? Doesn't it assume that, however a religion understands God, its understanding refers to the same God of another religion, perhaps even a religion that contradicts our religion?

For example, Buddhism typically believes that there are many gods, none of which is a creator. Hinduism, depending on the particular version, might affirm one god, or many, or that the world is god, or that there is no god.

How, we might ask, can these views be simply a "part" of a larger elephant, a larger truth? If the elephant is meant to represent God, then some religions claim there are many elephants, not one, while others would claim that there may be no elephant. Clearly the Buddhist parable cannot support its hope for the acceptability of religious pluralism.

The parable is correct, however, that we human beings are limited, so limited that it is not possible for any one of us, or all of us together, to gain comprehensive knowledge of God. That much is true.

This takes us directly to the reason why Christians claim that Jesus Christ is the only way to God. To adjust the Buddhist parable a bit, Christians claim that there is only one way to properly know the elephant. This claim is not a claim of personal arrogance. Nor is it a claim of unlimited knowledge. As we might expect by this point in the book, it is a claim that takes seriously the fact, and nature, of God's revelation.

As we have already seen, Christianity gives a transcendent reason to recognize the world as created, and human beings as specially endowed with God's image at creation. It is a transcendent reason because, as Scripture begins, we recognize that before all things began, God was. God, who transcends creation, creates all other things. He does not become those things, nor is he the "spiritual" side of humanity. He creates and bestows the gift of his image into all human beings.

Here we need to review what we have previously said. As we saw in chapter 6, the problems that ensue in God's good creation are due to Adam and Eve's rebellion against God. That rebellion included flaunting the very life that God had given them, a life that was unique as "image of God life." It was life that was meant to continue forever, had Adam and Eve obeyed. God promised them that if they did not obey him, they would die (Gen. 2:17).

When Adam and Eve disobeyed, they brought death to themselves and to the rest of creation (Gen. 3:14–19). That death was promised by God; it was what they deserved because they had rejected the life that God gave them in the Garden. Not only so, but because Adam was designated by God to be the head of the human race, his sin brought death on all who were born after him (see Rom. 5:12–21; 1 Cor. 15:47–48).

But death was not the last word from God. Instead, he promised, "I will put enmity between you and the woman, and between your offspring and hers; he will crush your head, and you will strike his heel" (Gen. 3:15). At the entrance of sin, the promise of God was that there would be enmity, or conflict, between those who would follow the progeny of Satan and those who would follow the offspring of the woman. In his commentary on Genesis 3:15, John Bunyan says,

> The seeds here are the children of both, but that of the woman, especially Christ (Gal 3:16). "God sent forth his Son made of a woman" (Gal 4:4). Whether you take it literally or figuratively; for in a mystery the church is the mother of Jesus Christ, though naturally, or according to His flesh, He was born of the virgin Mary, and proceeded from her womb: But take it either way, the enmity hath been maintained, and most mightily did shew itself against the whole kingdom of the devil, and death, and hell; by the undertaking, engaging, and war which the Son of God did maintain against them, from his conception, to his death and exaltation to the right hand of the Father.[6]

The Christian conception that Jesus Christ is the only way does not begin in the New Testament, as is sometimes thought. The fact that Christ is the only way to God actually begins in the Garden, immediately after the entrance of sin in the world.

The rest of the Old Testament testifies to this one exclusive Redeemer who will come to solve the problem that people produce and propagate. There are passages in the Old Testament too numerous for us to summarize that attest to this exclusive Redeemer. It might be best for us to see those Old Testament passages in Christ's own words.

On one occasion (John 8:48–59), Jesus was confronted by the religious leaders. They came to Jesus to accuse him of being someone "less" than they were, a Samaritan, and of being demon-possessed. If they were right, then Jesus had no right to "their" religion, and his spectacular works could be explained as Satanic.

Jesus uses some very strong words in response to these leaders. He calls them liars and tells them that, in fact, they do not know or trust in the true God (v. 55). As for their claim that they are children of Abraham, Jesus tells them (v. 56), "Your father Abraham rejoiced at the thought of seeing my day; he saw it and was glad."

Jesus is telling those who should have been experts in their religion that the very one they claim as their father, Abraham, rejoiced to see Christ's day. Abraham lived his life trusting God (Rom. 4:3) and looking forward to that "city with foundations," because its builder would be God himself (Heb. 11:10).

On another occasion (Luke 24:24–27), Jesus, after his resurrection, joins a conversation of two disciples who did not recognize him. The disciples were discussing the crucifixion of Christ, and they were dismayed that it had happened. Jesus says to them,

> How foolish you are, and how slow to believe *all that the prophets have spoken*! Did not the Messiah have to suffer these things and then enter his glory?' *And beginning with Moses and all the Prophets, he explained to them what was said in all the Scriptures concerning himself* [my emphases].

When we begin to read the entirety of Holy Scripture in light of these words of Christ himself, and to recognize that "all the prophets" were speaking of him, and that "all the Scriptures" (which at the time Christ spoke was only the Old Testament) were to be understood as revealing him, it can be readily seen why it is that Christians hold that Christ is the only way to God. Christ has been the only way to God since sin entered the world.

These summaries of Christ, together with the rest of Scripture's focus on Christ, give the proper context to Christ's words to his disciples in the upper room. The upper room was the place where Jesus took his disciples to prepare them for his death, which was imminent, as well as for their own ministries that would begin after his resurrection. He needed them to know what message they were to preach to the church when he was gone.

As Jesus counsels his disciples not to be troubled by the coming events, he also tells them that, as his disciples, they know "the way" where he is going (John 14:1–4). Thomas is confused by this, and he confesses that the disciples do not yet know the way. Jesus responds, "I am the way and the truth and the life. No one comes to the Father except through me" (v. 6).

No clearer statement of the exclusiveness of Christianity could be given. Jesus is talking about "the way" to eternal life, to heaven. "The way" might be understood to mean a path, perhaps a lifestyle that one must adopt in order to get to God. Jesus corrects that understanding. He is not talking about a path or a lifestyle. He is talking about himself. If someone wants to get to the presence of God, coming through Christ is the only way one can get there. He is the way.

This makes perfect sense when we recognize what it is that separates us from God and what the entire Bible, from Genesis 3 on, says about that separation. What separates us from God is not that we don't perform the proper religious functions, or that we don't live good enough lives. What separates us from God is our sin. And the only way that our sin can be overcome is if someone takes on the penalty of our sin, including death, and conquers it.

Only Christ can do that. No one else can. Because of our sin, "God made [Christ] who had no sin to be sin for us, so that in him we might become the righteousness of God" (2 Cor. 5:21). The serious and deep problem of sin, which began way back in the Garden, has one, and only one, remedy. God had to provide the remedy in himself. Sin has made us unable to defeat the enemy that we have created.

This is why the apostle Peter, as he was filled with the Holy Spirit and after the resurrection of Christ, says to the rulers and elders of the people: "Jesus is 'the stone you builders rejected, which has become the cornerstone.' Salvation is found in no one else, for there is no other name under heaven given to mankind by which we must be saved" (Acts 4:11–12).

Tolerance and Christianity

Before we move to some possible responses to what we have said, we need to deal with the "third sibling," tolerance. We can do this briefly, given what we have already said.

The central question with tolerance is why someone would extol its virtues. One of the reasons that we have grouped tolerance with its other two siblings—relativism and religious pluralism—is because it is very often thought that the reason we are to be tolerant is because truth is relative. No one religion, or position, is able to describe anything exhaustively. We should be tolerant of anyone else's view because it's just another version of truth.

But tolerance doesn't have to have these other two siblings. Instead, tolerance can be what it is in the context of the exclusive claims of Christianity. We can see this, again, in the life of Christ himself.

There can be no question that Christ lived a life that was

characterized by love and compassion. He had the power to calm storms and walk on water, to turn water to wine, and cause the dead to come to life again. As the one who had power over life and death, surely he had the power to destroy his enemies. Instead, he came to appeal to his enemies, to draw them to himself. It was while we were enemies that Christ died for us (Rom. 5:8).

Notice also, for example, how Christ responds to his enemies when others around him want to do them harm. When Jesus was being betrayed and arrested, Peter drew his sword and cut off the right ear of Malchus, a servant of the high priest. For Peter, it was time for war, and he was ready with his sword. What did Jesus do? "Jesus answered, 'No more of this!' And he touched the man's ear and healed him" (Luke 22:51; compare Matt. 26:50–54; John 18:10–11).

The way of Christianity is a way of tolerance. But that tolerance has its roots in the God who made and controls all that is. It is a tolerance that has its foundation in God's comprehensive control of all things, including the fact that his gospel is a gospel that alone brings and produces peace, not war.

Responses

Probably the most prominent response to Christian exclusiveness is some kind of inclusiveness. To be so exclusive, some will think, is to exclude so many others and all other religions.

There are a couple responses to this objection. The first response is that many other religions are just as exclusive as Christianity. Certain radical wings of Islam, for example, are so exclusive that they think it is proper to kill and destroy anyone who disagrees with them. Christianity does not have "exclusive" rights to exclusiveness.

But just because others are exclusive is no reason that all religions must be. Isn't inclusiveness a much more "loving" option because it, by definition, wants to include everyone?

In its book the *Bhagavad Gita*, Hinduism, through Lord Krishna, says, "In whatever way men approach me, I am gracious to them; men everywhere follow my path."[7] This sounds, at least on the surface, much more palatable. Why can Christianity not just include everyone, in whatever way, who is trying to follow a path?

Years ago it used to be fairly common to see religious people in various airports across the United States. On many occasions, I had conversations with these people while waiting for my flight. I remember one conversation with a woman who believed in some version of Hinduism. She was trying to explain to me the words of Lord Krishna and to convince me that everyone really follows his path.

The question I asked her seemed obvious enough to me. "If that is true," I asked, "then why are you here talking to me?" She wasn't exactly sure what I meant by my question. "Why does it matter what I believe, what the person next to me believes, even what you believe, if all of it is just Krishna's path to approaching him?" At that point, she handed me a flower and walked away.

For someone to be truly "inclusive" means that even those who believe that Christianity is exclusive have to be "included" in the universal religion.

But that is not what those who want to be inclusive believe. The example of the Hindu woman shows that those who think that everyone should be included also think that everyone should think that everyone should be included! When that is not true, then it turns out that the inclusive person is just as exclusive as the exclusive person. The person who is inclusive believes something, exclusively believes something, that others, maybe many others, don't believe. He believes that everyone should believe that all beliefs and religions get to the same place eventually. But it wouldn't be difficult to show that neither Buddhism, nor Hinduism, nor Islam, nor Christianity, nor a host of more "secular" beliefs are inclusive in this way. In the end, the inclusive person is just as exclusive as the ones they seek to oppose.

Conclusion

It is important to know—from a Christian perspective eternally important—what, or in whom, we believe. The fact that our belief is exclusive is no argument against it. It shows it to be in some ways like beliefs that all people hold. The important and central question is not what do I believe and who does it include. The central question is, Is my belief true? Christianity says it is true only when it has its focus in Jesus—the One who himself is the Truth.

Questions for Reflection

1. Can you think of a religion or person whose beliefs truly include all people? Why or why not?
2. If all people are exclusive in their beliefs, why is Christianity's exclusiveness so offensive to many people?
3. Aside from those given in the text, can you name other examples of God's tolerance toward those who are his enemies?

Recommended Reading

Piper, John. *Jesus: The Only Way to God: Must You Hear the Gospel to Be Saved?* Grand Rapids: Baker, 2010.

Ryken, Philip Graham. *Is Jesus the Only Way? Today's Issues.* Redesigned edition. Wheaton, IL: Crossway, 2012.

Zacharias, Ravi. *Jesus Among Other Gods: The Absolute Claims of the Christian Message.* Nashville: W, 2002.

Sproul, R. C. *Who Is Jesus? Crucial Questions.* Revised, expanded edition. Sanford, FL: Reformation Trust, 2009.

CONCLUSION

We have been thinking about various objections to Christianity and some responses that might surface in response to our answers. Clearly, it is not possible to cover all objections or to anticipate all responses that others might have to Christian answers. It might prove helpful, as we conclude, to provide a kind of road map to follow whenever objections to Christianity are given. A road map can keep us on the proper path and help us to navigate detours that might threaten to thwart our efforts.

One of the recurring themes that has been present in each of our chapters is the necessity for Christians to recognize the authority of God's Word. This is the only road that can dispel doubts. It is the only road that takes us to the proper responses to objections. This is basic to Christianity. It is so basic that it was the very first thing that Satan chose to attack when our first parents were in the Garden.

Moses begins the third chapter of Genesis by telling us that "the serpent was more crafty than any of the wild animals the Lord God had made" (Gen. 3:1). We should not pass over that statement too quickly. Why would Moses tell us such a thing?

One reason is that he is preparing us for the serpent's attack on God's truth. That attack, though it might be all too familiar to us, was "crafty." It was crafty because it began by asking a question—a question, perhaps, that may seem to be fairly innocent. "Did God really say, 'You must not eat from any tree in the garden'?" (Gen. 3:1).

This is, indeed, a crafty question. It might sound like the serpent (Satan) is there simply to gather information; he's merely curious. But we know that is not the case. He wants Adam and Eve to take a permanent detour off the road. He knows the road they're on will lead them to eternal life. He begins to steer them off the road by a mere "suggestion." He is asking the question to get Eve to start thinking that what God said might not be so authoritative after all.

Once Eve responds to the serpent, he moves in, literally, for the "kill." He flashes a sign on the road, telling them to exit immediately. He tells her that what God has said is a lie. He tells her that they can know God better if, instead of trusting what God says, they listen to him. But, as we know, he said what he did to keep Eve from knowing God better!

The subtlety of Satan's attack is stunning. Adam and Eve follow the "Exit" sign and get off the only road that would lead them to eternal life with the God who made them and who placed them in his Garden. Satan convinced them that what God said was not true. He convinced them to quit trusting God and to question his Word.

In *The Lion, the Witch and the Wardrobe*, C. S. Lewis gives us a marvelous picture of what it means to trust the Word of God, a picture that is the opposite of Eve's response to the serpent.

In Narnia, Edmund has shown himself to be a traitor. According to the laws of Narnia, every traitor belongs to the White Witch, and it is her right to kill him. Aslan is well aware of this law, so he meets with the White Witch in private. As they emerge from the private meeting, they hear Aslan's voice: "You can all come back," he said, "I have settled the matter. She has renounced the claim on your brother's blood." We find out later that the reason the claim has been renounced is because Aslan has agreed to be killed in Edmund's place. But the White Witch still has a question: "The Witch was just turning away with a look of fierce joy on her face when she stopped and said, *'But how do I know this promise will be kept?'* 'Haa-a-arrh!' roared Aslan, half rising from his throne; and his great mouth opened wider and wider and the roar grew louder, and the Witch, after staring for a moment with her lips wide apart, picked up her skirts and fairly ran for her life."[1] Here Lewis depicts for us the proper response to God's Word. Aslan's loud roar demonstrates God's response to those who would deign to question his authority. In effect, Aslan speaks volumes by saying nothing. He is saying that his word is bound up with his majestic character.

We can only imagine that such a "roar" was heard in the heavenlies when Eve decided that what God had told her and Adam was not true. The serpent in the Garden craftily deceived Eve into thinking that God's Word was not to be trusted. Perhaps Eve had asked herself the same question, "How do I know that God's promise will be kept?"

Since that time unbelief, in its multitude of forms, has sought to dismiss and reject what God has said. It has done this in various ways, but the end result is always the same. If you can convince yourself that God has not spoken, or that what he said is not clear, or that it is not possible to know that he has spoken, then you can convince yourself that you are your own master and have no responsibility to the God who made you and who provided salvation from sin.

Every objection that comes against Christianity has behind it the question of the White Witch, "How can I know that God has spoken, or that his promises will be kept?" Aslan's roar indicates

God's proper response to such questions—indignation. He needs no other response; he himself *is* the reason we can know. We can know because of the One who has spoken. If we refuse to trust God and what he has said in Scripture, no hope remains for us. Our lives, here and beyond, will be characterized by God's never-ending indignation.

For the Christian, this means that every objection comes with a refusal to trust what God has said. That refusal to trust God is always accompanied by a trust in something or someone else. In the end, it is accompanied by an unwavering trust in ourselves.

The only proper way to face the objections that come to us is by knowing God better. We do that when we know his Word better, and when we meditate on its consequences. For the Christian cannot take a detour or be distracted from the road we are on; it is the only road to eternal life. It is the road of Christ.

Years ago I was teaching a class on apologetics (defense of the Christian faith). One day after class, a woman approached me to tell me her story. She was a relatively new Christian. She was not a trained theologian and was not schooled in philosophy. Her roommate, however, was a woman who, she told me, was the first woman to hold a chair in philosophy at the local university. Her roommate was trying to convince this woman that Christianity was an illusion.

Through this course on apologetics, the woman explained, she had gained a new understanding of Scripture and its power. She recounted to me that she was now able to use what she had learned of the Bible to respond to her philosopher roommate's objections. She no longer doubted her faith, and she was equipped, in her knowledge of the Bible, to respond to the sophisticated objections that were coming her way.

This is the best and most productive way to begin to address objections that come against Christianity. It is not possible to know them all or to study them all. What is possible is to know God's Word better and better and to think about what God has said in light of the alternatives.

For example, as we have explained in this book, Christians believe that Christianity is true. That belief does not cause Christianity to be true. It does not make Christianity true. Nor is it a belief whose opposite can be just as true. When we confess Christianity to be true, we are also confessing that anything that opposes Christianity is, by definition, false. What do we mean by that?

In part, what we mean is that any objection to Christianity has no way to explain who people are, what the world is really like, what love is, why certain things are evil, etc. Because any objection to Christianity has no transcendent (i.e., biblical) foundation, it is off the road and trapped in a dark and confusing ditch. It has no way to see beyond its immediate context. It cannot reach up beyond its own situation.

So whether we know the details of every objection or not, we know that any objection simply denies the obvious. In wickedness, as Paul says, there is always suppression of the truth (Rom. 1:18). Every suppression of the truth is, by definition, a deception; specifically, a self-deception. This was Adam and Eve's problem (see 2 Cor. 11:3). Through Satan's temptation, they convinced themselves that what they knew was false. They knew that the God who made them and had given them the Garden was himself the truth. They knew, because they had experienced it, that what God said was exactly right. But Satan convinced them to suppress that truth and believe him.

All objections to Christianity will follow this same general pattern. It will come from those who know the truth of who God is, but suppress it. That suppression will include objections to what you believe. Those objections will try to move you away from trusting God and what he has said. This will always be the way your faith will be attacked.

If you are reading this book and you have not trusted Christ, here is the challenge: Take your objections and look at them from the perspective of what God has said in his Word. In order to do that, you will have to read his Word. In reading it, you should ask, "What does this say to my objections to Christianity?"

So many of the objections given against Christianity neglect to take seriously exactly what Christianity is. Oftentimes, as we have seen in a few examples in this book, they take what is most convenient for the purposes of the objection and pretend that such things are the sum and substance of the Christian faith. But once the Word of God is taken for what it is, there is no way that objections can stand scrutiny, and they will fade away like a mist.

In the end, whether a Christian or objector, a proper response to God and his Word can only come because, as we have seen in The Westminster Confession of Faith, "our full persuasion and assurance of the infallible truth and divine authority thereof, is from the inward work of the Holy Spirit bearing witness by and with the Word in our hearts."

The work of the Spirit accomplishes our change of heart. But the Spirit does not work by himself. He is committed to working "by and with the Word." It is our exposure to and our knowledge of that Word that moves us from being objectors to being those who alone can have hope in this world (compare Eph. 2:12 and Col. 1:5).

In reading and understanding God's Word, when the Spirit works in our hearts, we move from unbelief to faith in Christ. When we do, our faith is strengthened so that we might "demolish arguments and every pretension that sets itself up against the knowledge of God, and we take captive every thought to make it obedient to Christ" (2 Cor. 10:5).

NOTES

Introduction

1. The lecture can be found in C. S. Lewis, *C. S. Lewis Essay Collection and Other Short Pieces* (Fount, 2000), 21, https://openlibrary.org.
2. This creed can be found in a number of places, including http://www .reformed.org/documents/apostles_creed.html, from which this is taken.
3. See, for example, Justin S. Holcomb, *Know the Creeds and Councils*, Know Series (Grand Rapids: Zondervan, 2014).

Chapter 1: Why Believe in the Bible?

1. http://www.gospelherald.com/articles/60328/20151203/ancient-seal-of-old -testament-king-hezekiah-uncovered-in-jerusalem-this-is-as-close-as-we -can-get-to-touching-him.htm.
2. These historical facts are taken from, and expanded in, Steven B. Cowan and Terry L. Wilder, *In Defense of the Bible: A Comprehensive Apologetic for the Authority of Scripture* (Nashville: B&H Academic, 2013–07–01), 209ff., 229ff.
3. Norman L. Geisler, *Baker Encyclopedia of Christian Apologetics*, Baker Reference Library (Grand Rapids: Baker, 1999), 549–50.
4. Ibid., 532.
5. Dan Brown, *The Da Vinci Code* (New York: Doubleday, 2003), 231.
6. For a fascinating discussion and defense of Constantine's Christianity, see Peter J. Leithart, *Defending Constantine: The Twilight of an Empire and the Dawn of Christendom* (Downers Grove, IL: IVP Academic, 2010).
7. See Justin S. Holcomb, *Know the Creeds and Councils*, Know Series (Grand Rapids: Zondervan, 2014).
8. For a discussion of Marcion, see Justin S. Holcomb, *Know the Heretics*, Know Series (Grand Rapids: Zondervan, 2014), chapter 3.
9. B. B. Warfield, *The Inspiration and Authority of the Bible* (Philadelphia: Presbyterian and Reformed, 1948), 413.
10. Norman L. Geisler and William E. Nix, *From God to Us: How We Got Our Bible*. Revised and expanded edition (Chicago: Moody, 2012), 159, my emphasis.
11. *The Westminster Confession of Faith* (Oak Harbor, WA: Logos, 1996), chapter 1, section 5.
12. Ibid.
13. For an example of a mock dialogue between a Muslim and a Christian on this matter, see K. Scott Oliphint, *Covenantal Apologetics: Principles and Practice in Defense of Our Faith* (Wheaton, IL: Crossway, 2013).

Chapter 2: Why Believe in God?

1. Christopher Hitchens, *God Is Not Great: How Religion Poisons Everything* (New York: Twelve, 2007), 17.
2. Richard Dawkins, *The God Delusion* (Boston: Mariner, 2008), 5.
3. Richard Dawkins, *River Out of Eden: A Darwinian View of Life*. Science Masters Series, reprint edition (New York: Basic, 1996–08–23), 132.
4. Richard Dawkins, a review of Maitland A. Edey and Donald C. Johanson, *Blueprints: Solving the Mystery of Evolution," New York Times*, April 9, 1989.
5. See https://www.barna.org/barna-update/culture/713–2015-state-of-atheism -in-america#.VtSnhpMrKHr.
6. This quote is from *Tusculan Disputations*, I.XIII, and can be found at http://www.gutenberg.org/files/14988/14988-h/14988-h.htm.
7. John Calvin, *Institutes of the Christian Religion*, ed. John T. McNeill, trans. Ford Lewis Battles, vol. 1, The Library of Christian Classics (Louisville, KY: Westminster John Knox Press, 2011), 44.
8. Ibid., 43–44.
9. For a more detailed, exegetical discussion of Paul's argument in this text of Scripture, see K. Scott Oliphint, "The Irrationality of Unbelief," in *Revelation and Reason: New Essays in Reformed Apologetics*, ed. K. Scott Oliphint and Lane G. Tipton (Phillipsburg, NJ: P&R, 2007).
10. This essay can be accessed at https://www.andrew.cmu.edu/user/ jksadegh/A%20Good%20Atheist%20Secularist%20Skeptical%20Book%20 Collection/Why%20I%20am%20Not%20a%20Christian%20-%20Bertrand %20Russell.pdf.
11. Thomas Nagel, *The Last Word* (Oxford: Oxford University Press, 2001), 130–31, my emphases.

Chapter 3: Why Believe in Jesus?

1. Adapted from a sermon by Dr. James Allan Francis around 1926.
2. David F. Strauss, *The Life of Jesus*, 1868 (Book on Demand).
3. Benjamin B. Warfield, *The Works of Benjamin B. Warfield: Christology and Criticism*, vol. 3 (Bellingham, WA: Logos, 2008), 71–72.
4. Herman Bavinck, *Reformed Dogmatics: Prolegomena*, ed. John Bolt, trans. John Vriend, vol. 1 (Grand Rapids: Baker Academic, 2003), 344, my emphases.
5. Charles Hodge, *An Exposition of the First Epistle to the Corinthians* (New York: Carter, 1857), 175.
6. John Calvin, *Institutes of the Christian Religion*, ed. John T. McNeill, trans. Ford Lewis Battles, vol. 1, The Library of Christian Classics (Louisville, KY: Westminster John Knox Press, 2011), 133.

Chapter 4: Why Believe in Miracles?

1. C. S. Lewis, *Miracles, a Preliminary Study* (New York: Simon and Schuster, 1947).
2. Ibid.
3. David Hume, *An Enquiry Concerning Human Understanding*, The Harvard Classics, vol. XXXVII (New York: Collier, 1909–1914), part III, p. 11.
4. Taken from Hume's *Enquiry* in David Hume, "Against Miracles," in *Philosophy of Religion: An Anthology*, ed. Louis P. Pojman (Belmont, CA: Wadsworth, 1987), 261.
5. Ibid., 263.
6. Ibid.
7. Ibid.
8. Christopher Hitchens, *God Is Not Great: How Religion Poisons Everything* (New York: Twelve, 2007), 141.
9. Lewis, *Miracles, a Preliminary Study*, 134–35.
10. Ibid., 140ff.
11. Benedict de Spinoza, *The Chief Works of Benedict de Spinoza*, translated from the Latin, with an Introduction by R. H. M. Elwes, vol. 1 "Introduction," *Tractatus-Theologico-Politicus*. Revised edition (London: Bell, 1891), http://oll.libertyfund.org/titles/1710#Spinoza_1321.01_363, my emphases.

Chapter 5: Why Believe Jesus Rose from the Dead?

1. Josh McDowell, *Evidence That Demands a Verdict: Historical Evidences for the Christian Faith* (Orlando, FL: Campus Crusade for Christ, 1972), 270.
2. John Warwick Montgomery, *The Shape of the Past: An Introduction to Philosophical Historiography* (Ann Arbor, MI: Edwards, 1968), 237, my emphases.
3. Lewis Carroll, *Through the Looking-Glass*, (Kindle Locations 535–536), Kindle Edition.
4. See "UK Scientists: Aliens May Have Sent Space Seeds to Create Life on Earth," http://www.huffingtonpost.com/2015/02/03/aliens-send-space-seed-to-earth_n_6608582.html.
5. Michael Martin, *The Case Against Christianity* (Philadelphia: Temple University Press, 1991), 74.
6. Ibid., 75, my emphasis.

Chapter 6: Why Believe in Salvation?

1. *Unbroken* was also released as a movie in 2014, earning almost $170 million worldwide. The movie, however, ended prematurely, with Zamperini's return home from war.
2. Laura Hillenbrand, *Unbroken: A World War II Story of Survival, Resilience, and Redemption* (New York: Random House (2010), Kindle edition, locations 5991–994.

3. Ibid.
4. Ibid., Kindle, 6036–38.
5. This counsel that God takes with himself, as we discover in the New Testament, is a *triune* counsel among Father, Son, and Holy Spirit.
6. Hillenbrand, *Unbroken*, Kindle, 6137–138.

Chapter 7: Why Believe in Life After Death?

1. The poll was accessed at http://www.cbsnews.com/news/cbs-news-poll-americans-views-on-death/.
2. Christopher Hitchens, *Mortality*, reprint edition (Boston: Twelve, 2014), 14.
3. Philosophers such as Democritus and Leucippus (both fifth century BC) held this view. They believed that the body and the self (brain) were all of one material piece. Once the body died, the person no longer existed.
4. The desists in Butler's day were committed to a religion of nature. They did not believe in the need for Scripture in order to know God. They knew him "naturally," not through what God has said.
5. Joseph Butler, *Analogy of Religion, Natural and Revealed, to the Constitution and Course of Nature* (New York: Harper, 1860), 94.
6. Ibid., 84.
7. These quotations were accessed at http://americanhumanist.org/Humanism/Humanist_Manifesto_II.

Chapter 8: Why Believe in God in the Face of Modern Science?

1. Peter Harrison, *The Territories of Science and Religion* (Chicago: University of Chicago Press, 2015–04–06), 76.
2. From Boyle's *Theological Works*, quoted in Jonathan Irvine Israel, *Radical Enlightenment: Philosophy and the Making of Modernity, 1650–1750* (Oxford: Oxford University Press, 2001), 457.
3. Ibid., 519.
4. John William Draper, *History of the Conflict Between Religion and Science* (London: King, 1875), xi.
5. Andrew Dickson White, *History of the Warfare of Science with Theology in Christendom* (New Brunswick, NJ: Transaction, 2012), xxii.
6. Richard Dawkins, a review of Maitland A. Edey and Donald C. Johanson, *Blueprints: Solving the Mystery of Evolution*, *New York Times*, April 9, 1989.
7. Richard Dawkins, *The God Delusion* (Boston: Mariner, 2008), 51.
8. Charles Darwin, *The Origin of Species*, The Harvard Classics, vol. II, first edition (New York: Collier, 1909), 334.

Chapter 9: Why Believe in God Despite the Evil in the World?

1. Antony Flew, "Theology and Falsification," in Antony Flew and Alasdair C. MacIntyre, *New Essays in Philosophical Theology* (New York: Macmillan, 1964), 98–99.
2. Ibid.
3. Quoted in David Hume, *Dialogues Concerning Natural Religion*, second edition (London: 1779), 186.

Chapter 10: Why Believe in Christianity Alone?

1. Allan Bloom, *The Closing of the American Mind* (New York: Simon Schuster, 1987), 25–26, my emphases.
2. Bloom's solution has its own problems. He thinks a return to an ancient Greek idea of absolutes provides the cure. That solution is contrary to Christianity, but cannot be pursued here.
3. This statement is usually attributed to Richard Rorty, a philosophy professor at Princeton University.
4. Quoted from Louis P. Pojman, ed., *Philosophy of Religion: An Anthology* (Belmont, CA: Wadsworth, 1987), 497–98, my emphasis.
5. The actual quotation is in the form of a question, "Without God and the future life? It means everything is permitted now, one can do anything?" Fyodor Dostoevsky, *The Brothers Karamazov*, trans. Richard Pevear and Larissa Volokhonsky (San Francisco: North Point, 1990), 589.
6. John Bunyan, *An Exposition of the First Ten Chapters of Genesis*, vol. 2 (Bellingham, WA: Logos Bible Software, 2006), 437.
7. Quoted from Pojman, ed., *Philosophy of Religion: An Anthology*, 498.

Conclusion

1. C. S. Lewis, *The Lion, the Witch and the Wardrobe*, The Chronicles of Narnia (New York: Scholastic, 1995), 144, my emphasis. The latest movie from this book does a very good job of depicting this scene.

Know the Heretics

Justin S. Holcomb

There is a lot of talk about heresy these days. The frequency and volume of accusations suggest that some Christians have lost a sense of the gravity of the word. On the other hand, many believers have little to no familiarity with orthodox doctrine or the historic distortions of it.

What's needed is a strong dose of humility and restraint, and also a clear and informed definition of orthodoxy and heresy. *Know the Heretics* provides an accessible "travel guide" to the most significant heresies throughout Christian history. As a part of the KNOW series, it is designed for personal study or classroom use, but also for small groups and Sunday schools wanting to more deeply understand the foundations of the faith.

Each chapter covers a key statement of faith and includes a discussion of its historical context; a simple explanation of the unorthodox teaching, the orthodox response, and a key defender; reflections of contemporary relevance; and discussion questions.

Available in stores and online!

ZONDERVAN®
.com

Know the Creeds and Councils

Justin S. Holcomb

In every generation, the Christian church must interpret and restate its bedrock beliefs, answering the challenges and concerns of the day. This accessible overview walks readers through centuries of creeds, councils, catechisms, and confessions—not with a dry focus on dates and places, but with an emphasis on the living tradition of Christian belief and why it matters for our lives today.

As a part of the KNOW series, *Know the Creeds and Councils* is designed for personal study or classroom use, but also for small groups and Sunday schools wanting to more deeply understand the foundations of the faith.

Each chapter covers a key statement of faith and includes a discussion of its historical context, a simple explanation of the statement's content and key points, reflections on contemporary and ongoing relevance, and discussion questions.

Available in stores and online!

ZONDERVAN®
.com